THE SLOW COOKER KITCHEN

Nourishing, Reliable & Fuss-Free

150

GREAT RECIPES

★

CONTENTS

Introduction   4

Beef   6

Pork, Ham and Lamb   36

Chicken   72

Vegetables   112

Seafood and Fish   156

Bread, Cakes and Desserts   184

Index   222

INTRODUCTION

Slow cookers – those revolutionary dinner-cooking gadgets of the 1970s – are making a comeback! Their original target audience of new-to-work mums might have changed a bit since then but the device itself is just the same, and so are its benefits too. The 'set and forget' nature of slow cooking makes it the obvious choice for busy families, as well as hard-working professionals and students burning the midnight oil.

The other big benefit of slow-cooker meals is their use of budget cuts of meat, which come out perfectly tasty and tender after hours of cooking at low termperatures. So they're time-friendly and they're budget-friendly. What's not to love? The slow cooker fell out of favour in the '80s as some found its offerings to be lacking in flavour and texture. It doesn't have to be that way, and that's where this book comes in. In it, you'll discover a wonderful selection of slow-cooking recipes that are reliable, simple and deliver great results for you and your family.

This book kicks off with delicious recipes for that slow-cooking favourite, red meat. The slow cooker can transform the toughest cut of beef into something magical, so whether it's a stew or a roast you're after you'll find a recipe for it here. For a cold winter's night, choose from hearty stew recipes such as beef brisket ragu, the classic beef bourguignon, stroganoff, goulash or a spicy beef massaman curry. Everyday meals that are a cinch in the slow cooker include meatballs and lasagna, or for something a little different why not cook up the filling for a Philadelphia sandwich or sloppy joe?

Lamb-lovers will find plenty of good options here, including a classic roast lamb leg, which is mighty juicy and delicious cooked the slow cooker way, as well as a tasty lamb and bulgar stew and recipes for lamb shanks where the meltingly tender meat just falls off the bone. There are plenty of pork recipes in this book too, from slow-cooked ribs to sweet and spicy pork shoulder, to pork and apple casserole and that essential-to-impress recipe for pulled pork.

With the recipes in this book as your guide, you can use your slow cooker to recreate classic chicken dishes from around the globe including a rich and tasty chicken cacciatore, spicy chicken tikka masala, chicken teriyaki, Cajun chicken, red chicken curry, Moroccan lemon chicken, sweet and sour chicken or, for a Tex-Mex vibe, try the chicken tacos and chicken taquitos or the Tex-Mex soup. But you can also keep it super simple and use your slow cooker to make a whole roast chicken. Succulent and oozing with flavour, you might just be surprised how well it turns out. And to make things even easier on your hip pocket, you can use the slow cooker (and the carcass) to make a wholesome and flavoursome chicken stock, to use as a base for some many other meals.

Vegetarians and vegetable-lovers can put their slow cooker to good use too, creating interesting and tasty sides such as polenta, slow-cooked potatoes or glazed carrots, or soups, from everyday minestrone to a more elaborate borscht or lentil tamarind soup, or to make entire meals for all the family such as cabbage rolls, pumpkin risotto or vegetable stew.

Fish and seafood are not to be left out, with a full section in this book dedicted to interesting and tasty recipes for using these proteins as a base for dinner. Whether it's something simple, such as baked fish, coconut fish curry or prawn risotto, or something more challenging like bouillabaisse or stuffed squid, you'll find a good and workable recipe in this book.

Perhaps the biggest surprise about the slow cooker for those not in the know is its capability for producing amazing desserts and breads. If you're unconvinced, then give it a whirl, and see your slow cooker make light work of creating fluffy cakes and loaves, as well as creamy and buttery desserts. Keep it simple and try bread and butter pudding, baked apples, rice pudding or a chocolate slice in your slow cooker, or experiment with creme brulee, chocolate pudding or cinammon rolls. It's all doable with the minimum of fuss, time and cost, with the recipes in this book and your trusty slow cooker to hand.

BEEF

Beef brisket ragu	8
Beef taco soup	10
Lasagne	11
French veal stew	12
Italian meatballs	14
Beef stroganoff	15
Sausage and tortellini soup	16
Belgian beef stew	18
Massaman curry	19
Hearty beef stew	20
Sloppy joes	22
Philadelphia sandwich	23
Beef bourguignon	24
Corned beef	26
Irish stew	27
Osso bucco	28
Korean ribs (Galbi JJIm)	30
Mongolian beef	31
Chilli con carne	32
Easy pot roast	34
Beef goulash	35

BEEF BRISKET RAGU

INGREDIENTS

3 tbsps olive oil

1kg (2lb) beef brisket, cut into 3cm (1in) chunks

1 large onion, finely chopped

2 medium carrots, diced

1 celery stalk, finely diced

2 bay leaves

2 tbsps dried oregano

1 tbsp ground chilli flakes

3 garlic cloves, crushed

¾ cup (185ml, 6fl oz) beef stock

¼ cup (60ml, 2fl oz) red wine

¼ cup (60g, 2oz) tomato passata

2 tbsps tomato paste

Salt and pepper, to taste

METHOD

1. Heat 1 tablespoon of the oil in a large frying pan over high heat. Cook the beef in batches, for 3 minutes until browned, using another tablespoon of oil as needed. Transfer browned beef to the slow cooker.

2. Heat the rest of the oil in the same frying pan over medium-high heat. Add the onion, carrots, celery, bay leaves, oregano and chilli and cook for 5 minutes or until the onion is browned. Add the garlic and fry for a further minute. Transfer to the cooker.

3. Stir together the stock, wine, passata and tomato paste in a small bowl. Pour over the beef in the cooker and stir through.

4. Cover and cook on high heat for 4 hours or until beef is tender. Season to taste. Discard bay leaves before serving.

5. Serve with pasta or rice.

SERVES 4 ★ PREP 20MIN ★ COOK TIME 8HR LOW

BEEF TACO SOUP

INGREDIENTS

Olive oil, for frying

455g (1lb) minced beef

1 onion, chopped

1 x 400g (14oz) can pinto beans, liquid retained

1 x 400g (14oz) can kidney beans, liquid retained

1 x 400g (14oz) can whole kernel corn, liquid retained

3 tbsps tomato puree

2 cups (500ml, 1pt) water

2 x 400g (14oz) cans diced tomatoes

1-3 red chillies, to taste, seeded and chopped

½ bunch parsley, leaves picked and chopped (retaining some for garnish)

15g (½ oz) store-bought taco seasoning

Corn chips, to serve

½ cup (60g, 2oz) Cheddar cheese, grated, to serve

1 cup (250ml, 8fl oz) sour cream, to serve

METHOD

1. Heat the oil in a large frying pan over medium-high heat. Add the beef and cook, stirring, until browned all over. Drain.

2. Place the beef, onion, pinto beans, kidney beans, corn, tomato puree, water, diced tomatoes, chillies, parsley and taco seasoning in a medium slow cooker. Stir to combine.

3. Cook on low for 8 hours.

4. Serve topped with corn chips, grated Cheddar cheese, parsley and a dollop of sour cream.

LASAGNE

INGREDIENTS

2 tbsps olive oil

2 tbsps butter

1 onion, chopped finely

1 garlic clove, crushed

1 cup (30g, 1oz) parsley, chopped

½ cup (20g, ¾ oz) basil, chopped

550g (1¼ lb) minced beef

½ tsp salt

¼ tsp pepper

4 tbsps tomato paste

8-10 lasagne sheets

Cheese sauce

25g (1oz) butter

¼ cup (25g, 1oz) flour

1¼ cups (310ml, 10fl oz) milk

1 cup (125g, 4oz) Cheddar cheese, grated

¾ cup (90g, 3oz) Parmesan cheese, finely grated

METHOD

1. Heat the oil and butter in a large frying pan. Add onion and garlic and fry, stirring, for 3-4 minutes until starting to soften. Add parsley, basil and mince and cook for a further 5 minutes, stirring constantly. Season with salt and pepper and add the tomato paste. Set aside.

2. Heat the butter in a small saucepan and, when melted, stir in the flour. Gradually add the milk, stirring constantly, and bring to the boil. Add the cheese and stir until melted and combined. Remove from heat.

3. Layer the mince, pasta and cheese sauce in the slow cooker, finishing with a layer of cheese sauce. Sprinkle Parmesan on top.

4. Cover and cook on low for 5 hours.

FRENCH VEAL STEW

INGREDIENTS

3 tbsps plain flour

½ tbsp salt

½ tbsp pepper

1kg (2lb) veal stewing cubes

3 tbsps olive oil

3 carrots, sliced

6 Asian shallots, quartered

3 garlic cloves, minced

3 tbsps tomato paste

1 x 400g (14oz) can kidney beans

3-4 baby potatoes, halved

200g (7oz) mushrooms, quartered

1¼ cups (310ml, 10fl oz) chicken stock

1 cup (250ml, 8fl oz) red wine

4 bay leaves

2 sprigs of rosemary, leaves picked and roughly chopped

1 tbsp fresh thyme leaves (reserve some for garnish)

METHOD

1. Mix together the flour with the salt and pepper in a large bowl.

2. Toss the veal with flour mix to coat thoroughly.

3. Heat 1 tablespoon of the oil in a large frying pan over high heat. Cook the beef in batches, for 3 minutes until browned, using another tablespoon of oil as needed. Transfer browned beef to the slow cooker.

4. Heat the rest of the oil in the same frying pan over medium-high heat. Add the carrots, shallots, garlic and tomato paste and cook for 5 minutes or until the shallots are browned. Transfer to the cooker and stir through the beef.

5. Add the rest of the ingredients, cover and cook on low for 8 hours.

6. Discard bay leaves before serving.

7. Serve garnished with thyme leaves and some fresh crusty bread on the side.

ITALIAN MEATBALLS

INGREDIENTS

1 cup (125g, 4oz) breadcrumbs

2 tbsps Parmesan, grated

½ tsp salt

1 tsp pepper

2 large eggs, lightly beaten

1kg (2lb) minced beef

1 tbsp olive oil

Sauce

1 large onion, finely chopped

1 medium green capsicum, finely chopped

1 cup (225g, 8oz) tomato passata

1 x 400g (14oz) can diced tomatoes

2 tbsps tomato paste

2 large garlic cloves, minced

2 bay leaves

1 tsp each dried basil, thyme and parsley (or 3 tbsps mixed herbs)

1 tsp salt

½ tsp pepper

¼ tsp crushed red pepper flakes

METHOD

1. Place the breadcrumbs, cheese, salt and pepper in a large mixing bowl. Add the eggs and stir to combine. Next add the beef and mix together lightly but thoroughly. Shape into 4cm (1½ in) balls.

2. Heat the oil in a large frying pan until shimmering, then reduce heat to medium. Add meatballs and brown in batches. Drain and set aside.

3. Place the onion, capsicum, passata, diced tomatoes and tomato paste in the slow cooker. Stir in the garlic, bay leaves, herbs, salt, pepper and crushed red pepper flakes. Add meatballs, stirring gently to coat. Cook, covered, on low for 5-6 hours or until meatballs are cooked through.

4. Remove bay leaves. Serve with spaghetti.

BEEF STROGANOFF

INGREDIENTS

800g (1¾ lb) trimmed beef brisket, cut into 3cm (1in) pieces

Salt and pepper, to taste

2 tbsps olive oil

2 brown onions, thinly sliced

500g (1lb 2oz) button mushrooms, halved

4 garlic cloves, thinly sliced

2 tbsps plain flour

1 tbsp sweet paprika

1½ cups (375ml, 13fl oz) beef stock

1 tbsp tomato paste

1 tbsp Worcestershire sauce

2 tbsps sour cream

2 tbsps parsley, to garnish

METHOD

1. Season the beef with salt and pepper. Heat 1 tablespoon of oil in a large frying pan over high heat until shimmering. Add beef and cook in two batches, for 3 minutes each or until browned. Transfer meat to the slow cooker.

2. Heat the remaining oil in the same pan over a medium-high heat. Add the onion and mushrooms and cook, stirring ocassionally, for 5 minutes. Next add the garlic and flour and cook, stirring constantly, for 1 minute. Sprinkle with paprika and transfer the mixture to the slow cooker.

3. Combine the stock, tomato paste and Worcestershire sauce in a jug until smooth. Pour liquid over the beef and stir to combine. Cover and cook on high for 4 ½ hours or until beef is tender.

4. Stir in the sour cream and season with salt and pepper before serving. Serve with pasta or mashed potatoes and garnished with parsley.

SAUSAGE AND TORTELLINI SOUP

INGREDIENTS

Olive oil, for frying

455g (1lb) beef sausage, sliced

2 celery stalks, diced

1 onion, diced

2 carrots, diced

2 garlic cloves, minced

1½ tsps salt

½ tsp pepper

1 tsp paprika

4 cups (1L, 2pt) vegetable stock

2 x 400g (14oz) cans diced tomatoes

4 tbsps tomato paste

1 bay leaf

¾ cup (25g, 1oz) basil, roughly chopped

¾ cup (90g, 3oz) Parmesan cheese, grated

½ cup (125ml, 4fl oz) thickened cream

330g (12oz) frozen tortellini

½ bunch silverbeet, stems removed and leaves chopped

METHOD

1. Heat oil in large frying pan over a medium-high heat. Add sausage and cook, stirring, for 3-4 minutes until browned. Drain and set aside. Wipe pan clean with paper towel and heat a little more oil.

2. Add celery, onion and carrots and cook for 4-5 minutes until almost soft. Add garlic, salt, pepper and paprika and cook for a further 1 minute until aromatic.

3. Place the onion mixture, sausage, stock, tomatoes, tomato paste, bay leaf and basil in the slow cooker and stir to combine.

4. Cover and cook on low for 6 hours.

5. Remove bay leaf and discard. Remove sausage slices and set aside.

6. Puree the soup with a stick blender (or puree in batches using a stand blender). Add cheese and cream and stir to combine. Season to taste.

7. Increase slow cooker to a high setting. Return sausages to the slow cooker. Add tortellini and cook for 10 minutes, then add silverbeet. Continue cooking for 5 minutes until silverbeet has wilted.

8. Serve garnished with extra Parmesan and basil.

BELGIAN BEEF STEW

INGREDIENTS

2 tbsps flour

½ tsp salt

½ tsp pepper

800g (1¾ lb) chuck beef, cut into 3cm (1in) chunks

50g (2oz) butter

2 small onions, diced

2 garlic cloves, crushed

500g (1lb 2oz) button mushrooms, wiped

300g (10oz) small baby potatoes, peeled

1¼ cups (300ml, 10fl oz) dark beer (preferably Belgian!)

¾ cup (200ml, 7fl oz) beef stock

1 tbsp red wine vinegar

1 tbsp light brown sugar

1 tbsp Dijon mustard

1 tsp dried thyme

1 tsp tarragon

1 tsp dried rosemary

2 tbsps fresh parsley, finely chopped, for garnish

METHOD

1. Mix together the flour and salt and pepper in a large bowl. Toss with the beef until thoroughly coated.

2. Heat 1 tablespoon of the butter in a large frying pan over high heat. Cook the beef in batches, for 3 minutes until browned, using another tablespoon of butter as needed. Transfer browned beef to the slow cooker.

3. Heat the rest of the butter in the same frying pan over medium-high heat. Add the onion and cook for 5 minutes or until the onion is browned. Add the garlic and fry for a further minute.

4. Transfer to the cooker along with the rest of the ingredients. Cover and cook on low for 6 hours.

5. Season to taste and garnish with parsley.

MASSAMAN CURRY

METHOD

1. Place all the paste ingredients in a food processor or use a stick blender to process into a paste.

2. Heat half the oil in a large pan over medium-high heat. Toss the chopped beef in the arrowroot flour with some salt and pepper.

3. Cook the beef in batches, for 3 minutes until browned, using the rest of the oil as needed. Transfer browned beef to the slow cooker. Add the paste and stir to coat the beef.

4. Add in the onion, potatoes, beef stock and coconut milk and stir through. Cover and cook on low for 6 hours.

5. Just before serving, stir through the lime juice.

6. Serve with a sprinking of chopped coriander leaves, some star anise and cardamom for garnish.

INGREDIENTS

2 tbsps canola oil

1kg (2lb) chuck beef, cubed

1½ tsps arrowroot flour

1 large onion, sliced

3 large waxy potatoes, peeled and cut into chunks

1⅔ cups (400ml, 13fl oz) beef stock

1 x 400ml (14fl oz) can coconut milk, shaken

2 tbsps lime juice

Massaman paste

1 red onion, chopped

2 small red chillies, seeded and roughly chopped

2 tsps ground coriander

2 tsps ground cumin

1 star anise

½ tsp cardamom seeds

3 garlic cloves, crushed

2 lemongrass stems, white part finely chopped

2 tsps chopped ginger

1 tsp shrimp paste

3 tsps fish sauce

1 tsp palm sugar

10 stalks coriander

Salt and pepper, to taste

HEARTY BEEF STEW

INGREDIENTS

Olive oil, for frying

2 celery stalks, diced

1 onion, chopped

2 garlic cloves, crushed

800g (1¾ lb) beef chuck steak, cut into bite-sized pieces

2 tbsps plain flour

¼ tsp salt

¼ tsp pepper

4 bay leaves

1 tbsp thyme leaves

2 tbsps tomato puree

2 tbsps Worcestershire sauce

2½ cups (625ml, 20fl oz) beef or chicken stock

4 potatoes, cut into chunks

2 carrots, diced

1 red capsicum, finely diced

¾ cup (25g, 1oz) flat-leaf parsley, to garnish

METHOD

1. Heat olive oil in a large frying pan over medium-high heat. Add celery, onion and garlic and cook, stirring, for 5 minutes until just soft. Transfer to slow cooker.

2. Place the beef in a bowl and toss with flour, salt and pepper. Transfer to slow cooker.

3. Add the bay leaves, thyme, tomato puree, Worcestershire sauce and stock to the slow cooker and stir to combine.

4. Cover and cook on low for 8 hours or high for 4 hours until beef is very tender.

5. One hour before the end of cooking, add the potatoes, carrot and capsicum.

6. Garnish with parsley, to serve.

SLOPPY JOES

INGREDIENTS

Olive oil, for frying

1 small onion, chopped

450g (1lb) lean minced beef

1 tsp mustard

½ cup (125ml, 4fl oz) tomato sauce

¼ cup (60ml, 2fl oz) barbecue sauce

2 garlic cloves, minced

1 tsp Worcestershire sauce

1 tbsp cider vinegar

¼ cup (60ml, 2fl oz) water

2 tbsps brown sugar

METHOD

1. Heat olive oil in a large frying pan over medium-high heat. Add onion and cook, stirring, for 5 minutes until just soft. Transfer to slow cooker.

2. Place all the other ingredients in the slow cooker.

3. Cover and cook on high for 4 hours or low for 8 hours, stirring occasionally.

4. If mixture is not thick enough, leave the lid off the slow cooker for the final 30 minutes of cooking.

5. Serve on hamburger buns.

PHILADELPHIA SANDWICH

INGREDIENTS

1 tbsp olive oil

1 onion, sliced

1kg (2lb) round steak, thinly sliced

½ tsp pepper

1 garlic clove, crushed

1 green capsicum, seeded and sliced

3½ cups (875ml, 30fl oz) beef stock

6 bread rolls, sliced in half

12 slices of provolone or Cheddar cheese

METHOD

1. Heat the oil in a small frying pan. Add the onion and stir fry for 5 minutes until browned.

2. Rub the steak with pepper and garlic. Place it in the slow cooker.

3. Add the onion, capsicum and beef stock to the slow cooker and stir to combine all the ingredients.

4. Cook on low for 5-7 hours or until meat is tender.

5. Preheat the oven to 180°C (350°F, Gas Mark 4).

6. Place the rolls on a baking tray in the oven for 5 minutes or until crusty and lightly toasted. Remove from the oven and place a slice of cheese on both sides of each roll.

7. Remove meat mixture from the slow cooker and pile on top of the rolls.

8. Return to the oven for a further 5 minutes until cheese is melted.

BEEF BOURGUIGNON

INGREDIENTS

4 tbsps plain flour

½ tsp salt

½ tsp pepper

1kg (2lb) beef chuck steak, cubed

2 tbsps olive oil

1 onion, sliced

2-3 carrots, halved and sliced

225g (8oz, ½ lb) button mushrooms, whole

6 sprigs of thyme, leaves picked

3 garlic cloves, minced

2 bay leaves

1 cup (250ml, 8fl oz) red wine

½ cup (125ml, 4fl oz) beef stock

1 tbsp tomato paste

METHOD

1. Combine the flour, salt and pepper in a large bowl. Add the beef and toss to coat.

2. Heat the oil in a frying pan over a medium-high heat and add beef. Cook, stirring, for 4-5 minutes until browned all over.

3. Place the beef and all other ingredients into a large slow cooker.

4. Cover and cook on low for 6 hours or high for 3 hours, until meat is very tender.

5. Discard bay leaves before serving.

CORNED BEEF

INGREDIENTS

1.5kg (3lb 5oz) corned beef

½ cup (125ml, 4fl oz) malt vinegar

¼ cup (40g, 1½ oz) brown sugar

1 cinnamon stick

METHOD

1. Rinse the meat under running water. Transfer to the slow cooker.

2. Fill the slow coocker three-quarters full with water. Add the malt vinegar and sprinkle the brown sugar on top. Place the cinnamon stick in the water.

3. Cover and cook on high for 4 hours or low for 8 hours.

IRISH STEW

INGREDIENTS

460g (1lb) beef chuck steak

3 tbsps plain flour

½ tsp salt

¼ tsp pepper

Olive oil, for frying

1 onion, chopped

3 garlic cloves, minced

2 tbsps tomato paste

1 tbsp soy sauce

2½ cups (625ml, 20fl oz) beef stock

¼ cup (60ml, 2fl oz) Guinness (optional)

¼ cup (60ml, 2fl oz) red wine (optional)

2 bay leaves

4 small potatoes, peeled and chopped

2 carrots, chopped

Parsley, to garnish

METHOD

1. Toss meat with flour, salt and pepper.

2. Heat olive oil in a large saucepan over medium-high heat. Add beef and cook, stirring, for 3-4 minutes until evenly browned. Transfer to the slow cooker.

3. Place onion and garlic in the frying pan and cook for 3-4 minutes, until just soft. Transfer to the slow cooker.

4. Place tomato paste, soy sauce, beef stock, Guinness, if using, and red wine, if using, in slow cooker and stir to combine. Add bay leaves.

5. Cook on low for 7 hours or high for 4 hours until meat is very tender.

6. One hour before the end of cooking, add the potatoes and carrots.

7. Remove bay leaves. Season to taste with salt and pepper, and serve garnished with parsley.

OSSO BUCCO

INGREDIENTS

4 cross-cut, bone-in beef or veal shanks

1 cup (125g, 4oz) flour

Salt and pepper, to taste

Olive oil, for frying

1 onion, diced

2 carrots, diced

1 celery stalk, diced

2½ tbsps tomato paste

4 garlic cloves, minced

½ cup (125ml, 4fl oz) dry white wine

1 cup (250ml, 8fl oz) chicken stock

1 tbsp balsamic vinegar

1 tbsp oregano

2 sprigs rosemary

2 bay leaves

METHOD

1. Pat shanks dry using a paper towel. Place flour on a plate. Season beef with salt and pepper and dredge in the flour, shaking off excess.

2. Heat oil in a large Dutch oven or saucepan over medium-high heat. Add meat and cook for 5 minutes, until browned. Turn and cook for a further 5 minutes on the other side. Transfer to the slow cooker.

3. Add onion, carrots and celery to pan and cook, stirring occasionally, for 5 minutes until just soft. Add tomato paste and garlic and cook for a further 1 minute, until aromatic. Add wine and and stir. Transfer to the slow cooker.

4. Add stock, vinegar, oregano, rosemary sprigs and bay leaves to the cooker. Season with salt and pepper.

5. Cover and cook on low for 6 hours until meat is tender.

6. Remove and discard rosemary sprigs and bay leaves before serving.

KOREAN RIBS (GALBI JJIM)

INGREDIENTS

2.5kg (5½ lbs) short beef ribs, patted dry and cut into 4cm (1½ in) pieces

Salt and pepper, to taste

3 cups (300g, 10oz) dried shiitake mushrooms, quartered

3 small potatoes, cut into small 1cm (½ in) cubes

5 small carrots, cut into 1cm (½ in) lengths

1 cup (250ml, 8fl oz) chicken stock

Braising sauce

¼ cup (40g, 1½ oz) brown sugar

⅓ cup (80ml, 3fl oz) soy sauce

4 tbsps Japanese rice wine (mirin)

6 garlic cloves, crushed

4 spring onions, finely chopped

1 small onion, grated and squeezed to remove liquid

small piece ginger, peeled and roughly chopped

2 tbsps sesame seeds

2 tbsps sesame oil

1 medium nashi, peeled and roughly chopped

METHOD

1. Preheat an oven grill on high and arrange an oven rack about 15cm (6in) below the heating element. Line a large baking tray with foil.

2. Season the short ribs with salt and pepper on both sides. Place bone side up on the prepared baking tray and grill for 5 minutes. Flip them over and grill for 5 additional minutes. Place in the slow cooker.

3. Use a blender or stick blender to puree the sauce ingredients together into a rough sauce.

4. Add the mushrooms, potatoes, carrots and chicken stock to the slow cooker.

5. Add the braising sauce and stir to combine thoroughly. The liquid should completely cover the ribs and vegetables.

6. Cover and cook for 10 hours on low.

7. Season to taste before serving.

MONGOLIAN BEEF

INGREDIENTS

1kg (2lb) skirt steak,
cut into thin strips

¼ cup (30g, 1oz)
arrowroot flour

½ tsp salt

½ tsp pepper

2 tbsps sesame oil

2 garlic cloves, minced

½ tsp fresh ginger, grated

¾ cup (185ml, 6fl oz)
soy sauce

¾ cup (185ml, 6fl oz)
vegetable stock

¾ cup (120g, 4oz)
brown sugar

3 carrots, grated

4 spring onions, sliced
on the diagonal

METHOD

1. Add the meat, flour, salt and pepper to a large sealable bag. Shake vigorously to coat the steak slices in the flour mixture.

2. Add the sesame oil, garlic, ginger, soy sauce, stock, brown sugar, carrots and half the spring onions to the slow cooker and stir to combine.

3. Stir in the coated steak slices and stir through to combine.

4. Cook on high for 3 hours or low for 5 hours or until steak is cooked through and tender.

5. Serve over rice or noodles, garnished with remaining spring onion slices.

CHILLI CON CARNE

INGREDIENTS

2 tbsps olive oil

450 g (1lb) minced beef

1 onion, finely chopped

⅔ cup (150ml, 5fl oz) beef stock

½-1 tsp chilli powder

1 tsp ground cumin

½ tsp paprika

1 garlic clove, crushed

3 tbsps tomato puree

1 x 400g (14oz) can chopped tomatoes

25g (1oz) dark chocolate, broken into pieces (optional)

1 x 400g (14oz) can red kidney beans, drained and rinsed

½ cup (85g, 3oz) corn kernels

1 cup (45g, 1½ oz) fresh coriander, chopped

METHOD

1. Heat 1 tablespoon of the oil in a large frying pan. Add the beef and fry for 5-7 minutes or until well browned, stirring to break up any lumps. Remove from the pan with a slotted spoon and transfer to the slow cooker.

2. Add the remaining oil to the pan over a medium heat and gently fry the onion for 10 minutes, stirring occasionally, or until softened.

3. Meanwhile, place the stock in a small saucepan over a medium heat and bring almost to boiling. Remove from heat and set aside.

4. Add the chilli powder to taste, cumin, paprika and garlic to the frying pan with the onion and cook for 1 minute until fragrant, then add the tomato puree, hot stock and the tomatoes. Bring just to the boil, then carefully stir the mixture into the mince in the slow cooker. Cover and cook on low for 4 hours.

5. Stir in the chocolate, if using, kidney beans, corn and coriander and season with salt and pepper. Turn off the cooker and leave to stand for 10 minutes before serving.

SERVES 4 ★ PREP 5MIN ★ COOK TIME 4HR LOW/7HR HIGH

EASY POT ROAST

INGREDIENTS

1kg (2lb) beef chuck roast

1 onion, sliced

4-5 sprigs of fresh thyme

½ tsp salt

¼ tsp pepper

2 cups (500ml, 1pt) beef stock

METHOD

1. Place roast into slow cooker and surround with onion, herbs, salt and pepper.

2. Pour over the stock. Cover and cook on low for 6-8 hours or high for 3-4 hours.

SERVES 6 ★ PREP 20MIN ★ COOK TIME 7HR LOW

BEEF GOULASH

METHOD

1. Place the meat, ½ cup flour, salt and pepper in a plastic bag and shake to cover the meat.

2. Heat oil in a large frying pan over medium-high heat. Add the meat and cook in batches for 2-3 minutes each until browned. Drain off excess fat.

3. Place meat in the slow cooker. Sprinkle with paprika and cayenne, and stir to ensure evenly coated.

4. Add onions and garlic to slow cooker.

5. In a mixing bowl, combine tomato puree, diced tomatoes, Worcestershire sauce, mushrooms, brown sugar, mustard, lemon juice and beef stock. Pour over meat.

6. Cover and cook on low for 6 to 8 hours.

7. Mix the butter and 1 tablespoon flour to make a paste. Add to slow cooker and stir well. Cook on high for 15 minutes or until thickened.

INGREDIENTS

1.3kg (3lbs) beef blade steak, cubed

½ cup (60g, 2oz) plus 1 tbsps flour

1 tsp salt

¼ tsp pepper

1 tbsp olive oil

2 tbsps paprika

¼ tsp cayenne pepper

1 onion, diced

1 garlic clove, crushed

1 cup (225g, 8oz) tomato puree

1 x 400g (14oz) can diced tomatoes

2 tbsps Worcestershire sauce

6 button mushrooms, sliced

1 tbsp brown sugar

1½ tsps Dijon mustard

2 tbsps lemon juice

1 cup (250ml, 8fl oz) beef stock

1 tbsp butter

PORK, HAM AND LAMB

Roast lamb with garlic and rosemary 38

Sweet easy pork casserole 40

Pork and apple stew 42

Pork ragu 43

Glazed pork meatballs 44

Sweet and spicy pork shoulder 46

Chinese roast pork (char siu) 47

Slow-cooked pork ribs 48

Sausage jambalaya 50

Lamb rogan josh 51

Pulled pork 52

Easy lamb madras 54

Lamb shanks in gravy 55

Slow roast pork shoulder 56

Banh mi sandwich 58

Pea and ham soup 60

Vegetable and ham soup 61

Ham, egg and cheese tart 62

Spiced Apple butter 64

Plum jam 65

Spiced lamb and chickpea stew 66

Meatballs in tomato sauce 68

Lamb shanks in red wine sauce 69

Pork tenderloin with rice pilaf 70

ROAST LAMB WITH GARLIC AND ROSEMARY

INGREDIENTS

1 tsp salt

½ tsp pepper

8 garlic cloves, peeled and crushed

6 sprigs fresh rosemary, leaves chopped

1.5kg (3lb 5oz) trimmed, boneless leg of lamb, tied

2 tbsps olive oil

½ cup (125ml, 4fl oz) vegetable stock (or water)

METHOD

1. Preheat the slow cooker on a high setting for 20 minutes.

2. In a small bowl, combine the salt, pepper, garlic and rosemary together to form a paste. Rub all over the lamb.

3. Heat the olive oil in a large frying pan over a medium-high heat. Add the lamb and cook for 3-4 minutes, turning, to ensure even browning. Place browned roast into the slow cooker.

4. Pour the stock into the frying pan and bring to the boil. Pour hot stock over the meat.

5. Place the lid on the slow cooker and cook for 4-5 hours on high or 9-10 hours on low.

SWEET EASY PORK CASSEROLE

INGREDIENTS

500g (1lb 2oz) pork topside, cut into small chunks

1 onion, roughly chopped

1 yellow capsicum, diced

2 zucchinis (or squash), roughly diced

½ cup (75g, 3oz) prunes, halved

1 apple, peeled and chopped

1⅔ cups (400ml, 13fl oz) chicken stock

1 tbsp tomato puree

Handful of basil leaves (reserving some for garnish)

⅓ cup (100ml, 3½ fl oz) chicken stock

3 tbsps creme fraiche

METHOD

1. Place all the ingredients except the creme fraiche in the slow cooker and cook on low for 8 hours or on high for 4 hours.

2. Add the creme fraiche just before serving and gently stir to coat the meat.

3. Garnish with fresh basil leaves and serve on its own or with rice.

PORK AND APPLE STEW

INGREDIENTS

600g (1lb 5oz) pork topside, diced

1 tbsp arrowroot flour

Salt and pepper, to taste

2 tbsps olive oil

1 small onion, finely chopped

2 small carrots, grated

1⅔ cups (400ml, 13fl oz) chicken stock

¼ cup (50ml, 2fl oz) apple juice

1½ tsps ground fennel

2 red apples (jazz or sundowner), cored, peeled and cut into thick slices

500g (1lb 2oz) waxy yellow potatoes (such as bintje or Dutch cream), peeled and sliced 3mm (⅛ in) thick

2½ tbsps butter, melted

2 small garlic cloves, crushed

½ tsp salt

¼ tsp pepper

½ cup (125ml, 4fl oz) chicken stock

Sprigs of dill to garnish

METHOD

1. Toss the pork in a large bowl with the flour, salt and pepper.

2. Heat 1 tablespoon of olive oil in a large frying pan over medium-high heat. Add onion and fry for 5 minutes until soft. Add pork and fry in batches for 3 minutes to lightly brown. Transfer mix to slow cooker. Stir in the carrot, stock, juice and fennel. Cover and cook on low for 6 hours.

3. Stir in the apple, cover and cook on low for another 2 hours.

4. About 40 minutes before the pork will be ready, preheat the oven to 230°C (450°F, Gas Mark 8).

5. Gently mix together the potatoes, butter, garlic, salt and pepper. Place in a large, deep baking dish. Bake for 10 minutes, then flip the potatoes over and bake for another 10 minutes. Pour in the chicken stock and bake for another 12 minutes.

6. Serve the potatoes with the pork and garnish with sprigs of dill.

PORK RAGU

INGREDIENTS

2kg (4lb 6oz) boneless pork loin

1 tbsp rosemary, leaves picked and finely chopped

1 tsp dried mixed herbs

½ tsp salt

¼ tsp pepper

2 tbsps olive oil

2 x 400g (14oz) cans crushed tomatoes

¾ cup (185ml, 6fl oz) chicken stock

1 onion, diced

1 small carrot, diced

1 tbsp tomato paste

2 garlic cloves, minced

1 bay leaf

¼ cup (60ml, 2fl oz) red wine

450g (1lb) pasta, to serve

METHOD

1. Pat pork loin dry with paper towel and rub all over with rosemary, mixed herbs, salt and pepper.

2. Heat olive oil in a large saucepan over medium-high heat. Add pork loin and sear on both sides for 3-4 minutes until evenly browned. Transfer to slow cooker.

3. Place tomatoes, stock, onion, carrot, tomato paste, garlic, bay leaf and wine to the slow cooker.

4. Cover and cook on low for 8 hours or high for 4 hours.

5. Remove pork loin and shred the meat using two forks before returning to the pot until ready to serve.

6. Discard bay leaf before serving.

7. Serve with pasta.

GLAZED PORK MEATBALLS

INGREDIENTS

½ cup (60g, 2oz) breadcrumbs

½ cup (125ml, 4fl oz) milk

1kg (2lb) pork mince

1 egg, beaten

¼ onion, finely diced

2 garlic cloves, minced

¼ cup (10g, ¼ oz) sage, chopped

1 tsp cayenne pepper

1 tsp sweet paprika

Sauce

1 tbsp cornflour

1 tbsp water

1½ cups (375ml, 13fl oz) chicken stock

¼ cup (90g, 3oz) honey

2 tbsps soy sauce

1 tbsp tomato paste

2 tsps apple cider vinegar

METHOD

1. Preheat the grill to a medium-high heat and line a large baking tray with aluminum foil.

2. Combine breadcrumbs and milk in a large bowl and allow to sit for 5 minutes.

3. Add pork, egg, onion, garlic, sage, cayenne and paprika. Mix well using hands until well combined, then form into evenly sized meatballs.

4. Place on prepared baking sheet and place under the grill for 6-8 minutes, until lightly browned.

5. Transfer meatballs to the slow cooker.

6. In a small bowl, create a slurry by mixing together the cornflour and water until smooth. Add the other sauce ingredients and whisk to combine. Pour over meatballs.

7. Place a clean, dry tea towel over the top of the slow cooker and cover with the lid. This will absorb condensation. Cook on high for 2 hours or low for 4 hours until meatballs are fully cooked and sauce mostly absorbed.

8. Remove the lid and cook for another hour on low, gently stirring every 15 minutes.

SWEET AND SPICY PORK SHOULDER

INGREDIENTS

2 tbsps cornflour

½ tsp salt

½ tsp pepper

1kg (2lb) boneless pork shoulder, cut into 2cm (1in) cubes

2 tbsps canola oil

½ cup (125ml, 4fl oz) tamari sauce

½ cup (80g, 3oz) palm sugar

1 tbsp hot chilli sauce

3 tbsps sweet chilli sauce

3 garlic cloves, crushed

1 tbsp fresh ginger, grated

1 tsp Chinese five-spice powder

1 star anise

2 medium carrots, grated or julienned

1 small green capsicum, seeds removed, finely diced

½ cup (125ml, 4fl oz) chicken stock

Steamed rice, to serve

METHOD

1. In a large bowl, toss together the cornflour, salt, pepper and pork pieces. Coat the pork as evenly as you can.

2. Heat 1 tablespoon of the oil in a large frying pan over high heat.

3. Cook the pork in batches, for 3 minutes until browned, using the rest of the oil as needed. Set aside.

4. Add the tamari, sugar, chilli sauce, sweet chilli sauce, garlic, ginger, five-spice powder and star anise to a slow cooker and stir to mix thoroughly.

5. Stir in the carrots, capsicum and pork and coat thoroughly. Pour over the stock and cook, covered, for 8 hours on low.

6. Thirty minutes before serving, skim off some of the pork fat, then continue to cook for the last half hour without a lid. Remove the star anise and serve hot with rice.

CHINESE ROAST PORK (CHAR SIU)

INGREDIENTS

¼ cup (60ml, 2fl oz) soy sauce

¼ cup (60ml, 2fl oz) hoisin sauce

3 tbsps tomato sauce

3 tbsps honey (or maple syrup)

2 cloves garlic, minced

2 tsps ginger, peeled and grated

2 tsps dark sesame oil

½ tsp five-spice powder

1kg (2lb) pork loin roast

METHOD

1. Combine soy sauce, hoisin sauce, tomato sauce, honey, garlic, ginger, sesame oil and five-spice powder in a small bowl. Stir with a whisk to combine. Then coat the pork thoroughly with the mixture.

2. Place in a large ziplock bag and seal. Transfer to the fridge to marinate for 2 hours, turning occasionally.

3. Place pork and marinade in slow cooker. Cover and cook on low for 8 hours.

4. Remove pork from slow cooker using slotted spoon. Place the meat on a cutting board or work surface and slice. Serve with sticky rice and green vegetables.

SLOW-COOKED PORK RIBS

INGREDIENTS

1 onion, sliced

½ cup (125ml, 4fl oz) water

Olive oil, for frying

2kg (4lb 6oz) bone-in pork short ribs, trimmed

¾ cup (260g, 9oz) plum jam (see recipe page 71)

1 cup (250ml, 8fl oz) tomato sauce

¼ cup (40g, 1½ oz) brown sugar

2 tbsps red wine vinegar

2 tbsps Worcestershire sauce

2 tbsps Dijon mustard

¼ tsp ground cloves

¼ tsp allspice

METHOD

1. Place onion and water in the slow cooker.

2. Heat oil in a frying pan over a medium-high heat. Add the ribs and brown in batches. Transfer to the slow cooker.

3. Cover and cook on low for 6 hours until meat is tender.

4. Place the remaining ingredients in a saucepan over a medium heat. Cook, stirring, until combined and heated through.

5. Remove ribs from slow cooker. Discard cooking juices.

6. Return ribs to slow cooker. Pour sauce over top.

7. Cover and cook on high for 30 minutes or until sticky and well coated.

SAUSAGE JAMBALAYA

INGREDIENTS

1kg (2lb) boneless, skinless chicken thighs, cut into pieces

500g (1lb) smoked sausage, cut into 5cm (2in) slices

1 onion, chopped

1 red capsicum, seeded and chopped

2 celery stalks, chopped

3 garlic cloves, chopped

2 cups (500ml, 1pt) chicken stock

2 tbsps tomato paste

1 tbsp Cajun seasoning

1 tsp dried thyme

1¾ cups (275g, 8oz) long-grain rice

Chopped parsley, to garnish

METHOD

1. Combine chicken, sausage, onion, capsicum, celery, garlic, chicken stock, tomato paste, Cajun seasoning and thyme in the slow cooker. Cook on low for 5 hours.

2. Increase the temperature of the slow cooker to high and then add the rice. Cook for a further 30-45 minutes until rice has fully absorbed the liquid. Sprinkle with chopped parsley, to garnish.

LAMB ROGAN JOSH

INGREDIENTS

800g (1¾ lb) lamb fillets, diced

1 medium onion

210g (8oz) rogan josh paste

2 small green capsicums, seeded and diced

2 x 400g (14oz) cans crushed tomatoes

4 green cardamom pods, crushed

2 cinnamon sticks

2 bay leaves

Sprigs of coriander, to garnish

METHOD

1. Turn slow cooker to high. Place in the lamb and cook for 5 minutes. Stir, then add onion and stir again.

2. Add curry paste and stir to coat the lamb.

3. Add capsicum, then stir in the tomatoes and cardamom, cinnamon sticks and bay leaves. Cover and turn slow cooker to a low setting.

4. Cook for 7 hours, then serve with rice and naan, garnished with coriander.

PULLED PORK

INGREDIENTS

2 small onions, diced

2 garlic cloves, crushed

½ tsp ground cumin

¼ tsp ground cinnamon

1 tbsp chilli powder

2 tsps dried thyme

½ tsp salt

¼ cup (40g, 1½ oz) brown sugar

1 tbsp Dijon mustard

2kg (4lb 6oz) pork shoulder roast

1 cup (250ml, 8fl oz) barbecue sauce

½ cup (125ml, 4fl oz) apple cider vinegar

½ cup (125ml, 4fl oz) chicken stock

METHOD

1. Place onions and garlic in the bottom of a large slow cooker.

2. Place cumin, cinnamon, chilli powder, thyme, salt, brown sugar and mustard in a small bowl and stir to combine.

3. Pat the pork dry with paper towel. Rub with the spice rub all over the pork and place into the slow cooker on top of the onions.

4. Pour over the barbecue sauce, apple cider vinegar and chicken stock. Cover and cook for 10 hours on low or 8 hours on high, until the meat shreds easily with a fork.

5. Remove meat from the slow cooker, and transfer to a chopping block. Shred the meat using two forks. Return the shredded pork to the slow cooker, and stir the meat into the juices.

6. Serve inside toasted burger buns.

EASY LAMB MADRAS

INGREDIENTS

700g (1½ lb) diced lamb shoulder

1 tbsp olive oil or ghee

2 onions, peeled and sliced

2 garlic cloves, crushed

1 x 450g (16oz) jar Madras curry sauce

1¼ cups (300ml, 10fl oz) hot beef stock

3 tbsps natural yogurt

Salt and pepper, to taste

Handful freshly chopped coriander leaves, to garnish

METHOD

1. Place the lamb, oil, onion, garlic, curry sauce and beef stock in the slow cooker.

2. Cover and cook on high for 3½-5½ hours or low for 7½-9½ hours.

3. Add the yoghurt and cook for a further 30 minutes.

4. Season to taste, garnish with coriander and serve with rice.

LAMB SHANKS IN GRAVY

INGREDIENTS

½ cup (60g, 2oz) plain flour

1½ tsps salt

½ tsp pepper

4 lamb shanks

2 tbsps olive oil

2 onions, cut in wedges

1½ cups (375ml, 13fl oz) beef stock

½ cup (60g, 2oz) gravy powder

1½ tbsps rosemary, chopped

3 cloves garlic, finely minced

1 carrot, diced

METHOD

1. Place flour, salt and pepper in a large sealable bag. Place each shank in the bag individually and shake to coat well with the flour. Repeat until all shanks are coated in flour.

2. Heat the oil in a large frying pan over a medium-high heat. Add the lamb shanks, cooking in batches, and cook for 2-4 minutes until browned on all sides. Place the browned lamb shanks in the slow cooker. Add the onion wedges to the slow cooker.

3. Meanwhile, combine the stock, gravy powder, rosemary and garlic. Set aside.

4. Add the carrots to the hot frying pan and cook for 3-4 minutes until softened. Spoon the carrots over the lamb shanks.

5. Pour the stock mixture into the frying pan, scraping off any browned meat from the sides. Bring to a simmer and then quickly pour over the lamb shanks in the slow cooker.

6. Cover and cook on high for 2 hours. Reduce heat to low and cook for 6 to 8 hours longer.

SLOW-ROAST PORK SHOULDER

INGREDIENTS

1.5kg (3lb 5oz) pork shoulder

1 tbsp olive oil

¼ cup salt

1 tsp pepper

2 tsps ground coriander

2 tsps dried rosemary, ground or finely chopped

3 tbsps coriander seeds

8 cloves of garlic, minced

1 cup (250ml, 8fl oz) white wine

METHOD

1. Rub the pork roast all over with olive oil, salt, pepper, coriander and rosemary.

2. Heat a small frying pan over medium-high heat. Dry fry the coriander seeds for 4 minutes or until they start to brown. Remove the seeds immediately from the heat and set aside. Rub into the roast as well.

3. Put the roast, garlic and white wine in the slow cooker and cook for 6-8 hours on low. (To retain the firm texture of the meat, don't overcook it. Check at 6 hours. Timing will depend on the width of the cut of meat.)

4. Pre-heat the grill to medium-high.

5. Remove meat from slow cooker and place onto baking sheet lined with aluminum foil. Sprinkle with coriander seeds. Set under the grill until meat is nicely browned.

6. Remove from the grill and cover meat with foil. Allow to rest for 10-15 minutes before serving.

BANH MI SANDWICH

INGREDIENTS

Pork

1kg (2lb) boneless pork shoulder roast

½ tsp salt

¼ tsp pepper

1 jalapeno, diced

1 tbsp ginger, chopped

8 garlic cloves, minced

¾ cup (185ml, 6fl oz) soy sauce

¼ cup (60ml, 2fl oz) white vinegar

½ cup (80g, 3oz) brown sugar

Pickled carrot

½ cup (125ml, 4fl oz) white vinegar

½ cup (80g, 3oz) sugar

½ tsp salt

2 carrots, julienned

Sandwiches

½ cucumber, sliced

2 long baguettes, halved

1 cup (100g, 3½ oz) white cabbage, sliced

1 jalapeno, thinly sliced

Handful of coriander leaves

METHOD

1. Season the pork shoulder with salt and pepper. Place the jalapeno, ginger, garlic, soy sauce, vinegar and brown sugar into the slow cooker and stir to combine. Place the pork shoulder in the liquid.

2. Cover and cook on low for 8 hours or high for 4, until the pork is tender, rotating once during cooking process.

3. When the pork is ready, shred the meat. Strain and reserve the sauce.

4. Meanwhile, make the pickled carrots. In a medium mixing bowl, combine the vinegar, sugar and salt and stir until dissolved. Add the carrots and set aside to soak for 30 minutes. Drain and refrigerate until ready to use.

5. To assemble the sandwich, layer cucumber on the base of the baguettes, then top with the pulled pork, pickled carrots, cabbage, jalapenos and coriander. Drizzle with reserved sauce and serve hot.

PEA AND HAM SOUP

INGREDIENTS

455g (1lb) dried green split peas, rinsed

2 cups (300g, 10oz) thick cut ham, chopped

3 carrots, peeled and sliced

1 onion, chopped

2 celery stalks, chopped

2 large potatoes, peeled and cut into large chunks

2 garlic cloves, minced

1 bay leaf

6 cups (1.5L, 50fl oz) beef stock

Water, as needed

Salt and pepper, to taste

METHOD

1. Layer the split peas, ham, carrots, onion, celery, potatoes, garlic and bay leaf in the base of the slow cooker. Pour over the beef stock and don't stir.

2. Cover and cook on high 4 to 5 hours or on low 8 to 10 hours until peas are very soft. Thin out soup with water if desired. Add salt and pepper to taste.

3. Spoon into bowls, and serve hot.

SERVES 6 ★ PREP 25MIN ★ COOK TIME 5HR LOW

VEGETABLE AND HAM SOUP

INGREDIENTS

Olive oil, for frying

1 onion, diced

2 small carrots, diced

3 celery stalks, diced

2 garlic cloves, crushed

2 medium potatoes, diced

1 medium turnip, diced

6 cups (1.5L, 50fl oz) chicken stock

2 cups (500ml, 1pt) water

1 large ham bone

1 cup (200g, 7oz) barley

1 corn cob, kernels removed

2 Roma tomatoes, quartered

2 tbsps mixed dried herbs

1 tsp pepper

1 tsp salt

METHOD

1. Heat the oil in a large frying pan over medium-high heat. Add onion, carrots and celery and fry for 5 minutes, stirring often, until soft. Add garlic, potatoes and turnip to the onion mixture and cook, stirring ocassionally, for a further 10 minutes.

2. Transfer onion-potato mixture to the slow cooker. Add chicken stock, water, ham bone, barley, corn, tomato, herbs, pepper and salt.

3. Cover and cook on low for 5 hours.

4. Remove ham bone from soup and set aside for 5 minutes or until cool enough to handle. Shred meat from ham bone and stir into soup.

HAM, EGG AND CHEESE TART

INGREDIENTS

1 tbsp olive oil

1 large onion, finely chopped

2 garlic cloves, crushed

3 sheets shortcrust pastry (store-bought or homemade)

9 eggs, beaten

1¼ cups (310ml, 10fl oz) thickened cream

½ cup (60g, 2oz) mozzarella cheese, grated

¾ cup (90g, 3oz) ham, chopped

½ tsp Dijon mustard

½ tsp salt

¾ cup (60g, 2oz) Cheddar cheese, grated

¼ cup (35g, 1¼ oz) flat-leaf parsley, chopped

¼ cup (35g, 1¼ oz) fresh dill, chopped

METHOD

1. Heat the oil in a small frying pan over medium-high heat. Add onion and cook for 5 minutes, until soft. Add garlic and cook for 1-2 minutes until aromatic.

2. Grease and line the base and sides of the slow cooker with baking paper, leaving an overhang at the top.

3. Using the slow cooker lid as a guide, cut a piece of pastry approximately 7cm (3in) larger than the lid.

4. Gently press the pastry into the base and up the sides of the slow cooker. Use a knife to gently score and remove excess pastry and to provide a clean crust.

5. In a large mixing bowl, combine the eggs, cream, mozzarella cheese, ham, mustard and salt and whisk together. Add the onion and garlic and stir to combine. Pour the mixture into the prepared crust. Sprinkle with Cheddar cheese.

6. Place a clean, dry tea towel over the top of the slow cooker and cover with the lid. This will absorb condensation.

7. Cook on high for 3-4 hours, until the edges of the crust are brown and the centre of the tart is set.

8. Lift the entire tart out of the slow cooker by the edges of the baking paper. Cool for 10 minutes before serving.

9. Garnish with parsley and dill

SPICED APPLE BUTTER

INGREDIENTS

1 cup (155g, 5oz)
packed brown sugar

½ cup (155g, 5oz)
maple syrup

¼ cup (60ml, 2fl oz)
apple cider

1 tbsp ground cinnamon

½ tsp ground cloves

¼ tsp ground nutmeg

12 red apples, (pink lady
or sundowner) peeled
and cut into chunks

METHOD

1. Combine all ingredients in the slow cooker.

2. Cover and cook on low 10 hours or until apples are very tender.

3. Place a large fine-mesh sieve over a large mixing bowl. Add half of the apple pulp and press through with the back of a wooden spoon. Discard pulp. Repeat with the other half of the mixture.

4. Return apple mixture to slow cooker. Cook, uncovered, on high for 1½ hours or until mixture has thickened to a butter-like consistency.

5. Store in a glass jar in the refrigerator for up to 1 week.

PLUM JAM

INGREDIENTS

2kg (4lb 6oz) plums (preferably damson)

Water (as needed)

1 cup (150g, 5oz) light brown sugar

METHOD

1. Wash the plums in a colander under cold running water, remove any stalks and leaves as well as any bruised or rotten fruit.

2. To stone the plums, cut in half and remove the stone. Place the plum halves in the slow cooker, cover and cook on low for 12-16 hours. It shouldn't need any water, but add a couple of tablespoons of the jam is too thick.

3. Near the end of the cooking process, stir frequently. In the last 4 hours, stir through the brown sugar.

4. Once cooked, you can push it through a strainer to remove skin or use it as is.

5. Pour the jam into sterilised jars and seal.

6. Place the jars in boiling water for 10 minutes to sterilise further. (Or you can run them through a hot cycle in the dishwasher.) This will allow the jam to keep for up to 6 months.

SPICED LAMB AND CHICKPEA STEW

INGREDIENTS

2 tbsps olive oil

1 medium onion, chopped

2 ribs celery, finely chopped

2 garlic cloves, crushed

700g (1½ lb) lamb fillet, cut into 2cm (1in) chunks

1 x 400g (14oz) can chickpeas, rinsed and drained

1 x 400g (14oz) can diced tomatoes

1 small carrot, diced

1½ cups (375ml, 13fl oz) vegetable stock

2 tbsps preserved lemon, chopped

2 bay leaves

1½ tsps ground cumin

1½ tsps ground coriander

1 tsp cinnamon powder

½ tsp allspice

1 tbsp lemon juice

3 cups (750ml, 24fl oz) water

2 tbsps olive oil

½ tsp salt

¾ cup (75g, 3oz) redcurrants (optional)

½ cup (10g, ¼ oz) flat-leaf parsley leaves, to garnish

METHOD

1. Heat half the oil in a small frying pan over medium-high heat. Add the onion and fry for 5 minutes until softened and browned. Add the celery and garlic and fry for a further minute.

2. Add the rest of the oil then cook the lamb in batches, for 3 minutes until browned. Transfer the lamb and onion mixture to the slow cooker as you go.

3. Add the chickpeas, tomatoes, carrot, stock, lemon, bay leaves, cumin, coriander, cinnamon, allspice and lemon juice. Cook on low for 8 hours.

4. Remove the lid for the last hour if the stew has too much liquid.

5. Fifteen minutes before the stew is ready, prepare the couscous.

6. Bring the water, olive oil and salt to a boil in a large saucepan. Turn off the heat and pour in the couscous and stir to mix through. Cover to allow couscous steam for 5 minutes. Fluff with a fork before serving.

7. Just before serving, stir the redcurrants, if using, through the lamb stew.

8. Serve with couscous and garnish with parsley leaves.

MEATBALLS IN TOMATO SAUCE

INGREDIENTS

Meatballs

900g (2lb) minced pork

2 eggs, beaten

4 garlic cloves, crushed

½ cup (60g, 2oz) fresh breadcrumbs

1½ tbsps dried mixed herbs

1 tsp ground chilli powder

4 tbsps water

¼ cup (25g, 1oz) Parmesan cheese, grated

¼ cup (25g, 1oz) carrot, grated

Salt and pepper, to taste

Sauce

¼ cup (60ml, 2fl oz) olive oil

1 large onion, finely chopped

3 garlic cloves, crushed

4 cups (1L, 2pt) passata

2 x 400g (14oz) cans diced tomatoes, undrained

¾ cup (170g, 6oz) tomato paste

½ cup (125ml, 4fl oz) vegetable stock

1 tsp light brown sugar

¼ cup (10g, ¼ oz) flat-leaf parsley, chopped, for garnish

METHOD

1. In a large mixing bowl, combine all the meatball ingredients including a couple of good grinds of salt and pepper. Shape into 24 round meatballs. Set aside.

2. Heat the oil in a medium frying pan over medium-high heat.

3. Add the onion and fry for 5 minutes until softened and browned. Add the garlic and fry for a further minute.

4. Mix together the onion, garlic and the rest of the sauce ingredients in the slow cooker.

5. Place the meatballs in the cooker in the sauce.

6. Cook on low for 8 hours.

7. Serve garnished with chopped parsley.

LAMB SHANKS IN RED WINE SAUCE

INGREDIENTS

2 tbsps olive oil

4 lamb shanks

3 garlic cloves, crushed

1 cup (250ml, 8fl oz) dry red wine, such as Cabernet Sauvignon or Merlot

½ cup (125ml, 4fl oz) beef stock

3 tbsps wholegrain mustard

1 tbsp dried rosemary, finely chopped

1 tsp balsamic vinegar

¼ tsp cinnamon

1½ tsps salt

½ tsp pepper

2 rosemary sprigs, to garnish

¼ cup (10g, ¼ oz) fresh flat-leaf parsley, finely chopped, to garnish

METHOD

1. Heat the oil in a large frying pan over medium-high heat and quickly brown the lamb shanks on all sides for about 2 minutes.

2. Place the shanks to the slow cooker, then add the rest of the ingredients except the garnish to the cooker.

3. Cook on high for 2 hours, then reduce the cooker heat to low and cook for 7 hours.

4. Serve the shanks on mashed potato, garnished with rosemary and parsley.

PORK TENDERLOIN WITH RICE PILAF

INGREDIENTS

2 tbsps olive oil

2 large onions, halved and thinly sliced

2 garlic cloves, minced

1kg (2lb) pork tenderloin, cut into large pieces

¾ cup (200ml, 7fl oz) vegetable stock

½ cup (95g, 3oz) dried apricots, finely chopped

½ packet (20g, ¾ oz) dried French onion soup mix

¼ cup (30g, 1oz) slivered almonds, finely chopped

2 tbsps Dijon mustard

Salt and pepper, to taste

1½ cups (235g, 7oz) rice, rinsed and drained

3 cups (750ml, 24fl oz) cold water

1 cup (55g, 2oz) radishes, thinly sliced

½ cup (10g, ¼ oz) flat-leaf parsley leaves, to garnish

METHOD

1. Heat the oil in a medium frying pan over medium-high heat.

2. Add the onion and fry for 5 minutes until softened and browned. Add the garlic and fry for a further minute.

3. Add to the slow cooker along with the pork, stock, apricots, soup mix, almonds and Dijon mustard along with a couple of good grinds of salt and pepper. Stir to combine thoroughly.

4. Cover and cook on low for 8 hours.

5. If the mixture has too much liquid, remove the lid for the last hour. Season to taste before serving.

6. Place the rice in a large saucepan with the water. Bring to a boil, reduce the heat, cover and simmer for 12 minutes or until the rice is cooked. Season the rice with salt and pepper.

7. Serve the pork on the rice with the sliced radishes on the side and garnished with parsley leaves.

CHICKEN

Vietnamese chicken pho soup 74

Honey rosemary chicken 76

Whole roast chicken 77

Tex-mex chicken soup 78

Orange sesame drumsticks 80

Chicken cacciatore 81

Chicken coconut curry 82

Coq au vin 84

Cajun chicken with rice 85

Honey BBQ chicken tacos 86

Chicken stroganoff 88

Apricot chicken 89

Chicken and mushroom pot pies 90

Moroccan lemon chicken 92

Chicken taquitos 94

Paprika chicken 95

Red chicken curry 96

Chicken with tomatoes and herbs 98

Chicken drumsticks with capsicum 99

Glazed duck with figs 100

Chicken tikka masala 102

Homemade chicken stock 103

Chicken with rice and sultanas 104

Sweet and sour chicken 106

Chicken teriyaki 108

Maple dijon chicken 109

Farmhouse chicken broth with dumplings 110

VIETNAMESE CHICKEN PHO SOUP

INGREDIENTS

8 cups (2L, 4pt) chicken stock

2 tbsps brown sugar

2 tbsps fish sauce

8 whole star anise

6 whole cloves

1 tbsp coriander seeds

Small piece fresh ginger, thinly sliced

1 cinnamon stick

2 chicken breasts (bone in), trimmed and skin removed

150g (5oz) rice noodles

4 spring onions, finely sliced

225g (8oz) bean sprouts

1 cup (30g, 1oz) basil leaves, chopped

1 cup (30g, 1oz) mint leaves, chopped

1 cup (30g, 1oz) coriander leaves, chopped

1 red chilli, sliced

1 lime, wedged

METHOD

1. Place stock, brown sugar, fish sauce, star anise, cloves, coriander seeds, ginger and cinnamon stick in a large slow cooker. Add chicken breasts. Cover and cook on high for 4 hours or low for 6 hours.

2. Remove the chicken and set aside to cool slightly.

3. Remove star anise, cloves, coriander seeds and cinammon from slow cooker with a slotted spoon. Discard.

4. Add noodles and spring onions to the slow cooker. Cover and cook on high for 30 minutes.

5. When chicken is cool enough to handle, coarsely shred meat from the bone using a fork. Return to the slow cooker to reheat for 5 minutes.

6. Ladle soup into bowls and serve with bean sprouts, fresh herbs, sliced chilli and lime wedges.

HONEY ROSEMARY CHICKEN

INGREDIENTS

8 chicken drumsticks

4 garlic cloves, minced

½ cup (180g, 6oz) honey

2 tbsps tomato paste

½ cup (125ml, 4fl oz) soy sauce

2 tsps rosemary, finely chopped

1 tsp pepper

½ tsp red chilli flakes (optional)

3 cups (495g, 1lb 1oz) cooked rice

METHOD

1. Arrange chicken drumsticks on the bottom of your slow cooker.

2. In a mixing bowl, combine garlic, honey, tomato paste, soy sauce, rosemary, pepper and chilli flakes, if using, and stir until thoroughly combined.

3. Pour the sauce over the chicken drumsticks.

4. Cover and cook on low for 6 hours or for 4 hours on high.

5. Transfer chicken to a serving plate. Serve on rice, garnished with fresh rosemary sprigs.

WHOLE ROAST CHICKEN

INGREDIENTS

2 large onions, ends sliced off and halved

2 medium lemons, washed and halved

1 whole roasting chicken

3 garlic cloves, crushed

2 tbsps olive oil

1 tbsp salt

Pepper, to taste

METHOD

1. Place the onions in the bottom of the slow cooker, with the larger cut end on the bottom.

2. Stuff 3 of the lemon halves into the chicken cavity. Squeeze the rest over the chicken.

3. Rub the chicken all over with the garlic, oil, salt and a couple of good grinds of pepper.

4. Cover and cook on low 8 hours. In the last 15 minutes of cooking, preheat the oven to 230°C (450°F, Gas Mark 6).

5. Once the chicken is finished cooking in the slow cooker, remove it to a baking dish. Drizzle a small amount of oil over the chicken, then place in the oven for 15 minutes to crisp up.

6. Remove from oven and serve hot.

TEX-MEX CHICKEN SOUP

INGREDIENTS

2 tbsps butter

2 tbsps plain flour

4 cups (1L, 2pt) chicken stock

½ cup (125ml, 4fl oz) milk

1 x 400g (14oz) can creamed corn

2 cups (550g, 1¼ lb) tomato salsa

½ small onion, finely chopped

1 tbsp ground cumin

1 tbsp ground oregano

2 tsps cayenne pepper

1 x 400g (14oz) can cannellini beans, rinsed and drained

Salt and pepper, to taste

2 large chicken breasts

2 cups (55g, 2oz) plain corn chips, crushed

1 cup (125g, 4oz) Edam or Cheddar cheese, grated

1 avocado, sliced

¼ cup (10g, ¼ oz) fresh coriander, finely chopped

METHOD

1. Melt butter in a large saucepan over medium-low heat. Stir in the flour for 1 minute, keep stirring until smooth. Keep stirring and gradually add ½ cup chicken stock and ½ cup milk, until smooth. Bring to a boil, then stir in the rest of the stock, creamed corn and salsa. Pour into the slow cooker.

2. Add the onion, cumin, oregano, cayenne, cannellini beans and a couple of good grinds of salt and pepper and stir through.

3. Place the chicken breasts in the mixture.

4. Cover and cook on low for 8 hours.

5. Remove the chicken breasts and use two forks to shred into small pieces.

6. Use a blender or stick blender to puree the soup until smooth.

7. Return the chicken to the soup and stir through. Season to taste.

8. Serve with crushed corn chips stirred through, a handful of cheese on top and garnished with avocado slices and coriander.

ORANGE SESAME DRUMSTICKS

INGREDIENTS

⅓ cup (115g, 4oz) honey

2 tsps sesame oil

1 orange, zested and juiced

3 tbsps soy sauce

3 garlic cloves, minced

Small piece ginger, peeled and minced

1 tbsp rice wine vinegar

¼ tsp chilli flakes

1 tbsp toasted sesame seeds

Olive oil, for frying

8 chicken drumsticks

2 tbsps parsley, chopped, to garnish

2 tsps sesame seeds, to garnish

METHOD

1. In a medium bowl, combine honey, sesame oil, orange zest, orange juice, soy sauce, garlic, ginger, vinegar, chilli flakes and sesame seeds. Set aside.

2. Heat oil in a large frying pan over medium-high. Add chicken and cook for 3 minutes each side, until golden brown. Transfer to the slow cooker with the sauce.

3. Cover and cook on low for 8 hours.

4. Remove drumsticks and transfer to a plate. Cover with aluminium foil to keep warm.

5. Carefully pour the liquid from the slow cooker into a medium frying pan. Bring to a boil over high heat and cook for 5 minutes until sauce has reduced and thickened. Pour the sauce over the drumsticks and stir to coat.

6. Serve, garnished with parsley and sesame seeds.

CHICKEN CACCIATORE

INGREDIENTS

Olive oil, for frying

6 chicken pieces (leg and thigh), skin on

1 onion, chopped

2 garlic cloves, minced

1 celery stalk, chopped

1 red capsicum, deseeded and diced

15 small button mushrooms, sliced

1 cup (250ml, 8fl oz) dry white wine

2 x 400g (14oz) cans diced tomatoes

½ tsp salt

¼ tsp pepper

¼ tsp chilli flakes

20 Kalamata olives

¼ cup (10g, ¼oz) basil leaves, chopped

Basil leaves, to garnish

METHOD

1. Heat oil in a large frying pan over medium-high. Add chicken and cook for 3 minutes each side, until golden brown. Transfer to the slow cooker.

2. Place the onion, garlic, celery, capsicum and mushrooms in the slow cooker.

3. Deglaze the pan with the white wine and cook for 1-2 minutes, scraping down the sides. Pour mixture into the slow cooker.

4. Add tomatoes, salt, pepper and chilli flakes and stir to mix.

5. Cover and cook on low for 8 hours or high for 4 hours.

6. Add olives and chopped basil and stir. Cook for a further 1 hour, uncovered.

7. Serve, garnished with basil leaves.

CHICKEN COCONUT CURRY

INGREDIENTS

Curry paste

2 onions, roughly chopped

4 garlic cloves, crushed

2 green chillies, seeded and chopped

Small piece fresh ginger, peeled and roughly chopped

2 lemongrass stalks, white part roughly chopped

3 tbsps water

Curry

Olive oil, for frying

2 tsps garam masala

2 tsps ground coriander

2 tsps ground cumin

2 tsps ground turmeric

1 x 400ml (14fl oz) coconut milk

4 boneless chicken thighs, chopped into bite-sized pieced

2 long red chillies (optional)

2 carrots, diced

2 potatoes, diced

2 zucchinis, diced

METHOD

1. Place the onions, garlic, chillies, ginger, lemongrass and water in a food processor (or blender) and whizz until a rough paste forms.

2. Heat oil in a frying pan over medium-high heat. Add paste and fry for 1-2 minutes until aromatic. Add the garam masala, ground coriander, cumin and turmeric and fry for a further 3-4 minutes. Add a spash of coconut milk to deglaze the pan and transfer to a medium slow cooker.

3. Pour in the remainder of the coconut milk and stir to combine. Add the chicken and red chillies, if using.

4. Cover and cook on low for 4 hours.

5. Add carrot, potato and zucchini and cook for a further 1 hour.

COQ AU VIN

INGREDIENTS

2 tbsps olive oil

6 bone-in chicken pieces (breast and leg)

4 slices bacon

3 cups (750ml, 24fl oz) red wine

1 cup (250ml, 8fl oz) chicken stock

3 garlic cloves, smashed

2 sprigs tarragon

3 sprigs thyme

1 bay leaf

½ tsp salt

¼ tsp pepper

1 small onion, quartered

6 small carrots, quartered

300g (10oz) button mushrooms

METHOD

1. Heat oil in a large frying pan over medium-high heat. Add chicken and cook for 3 minutes each side, until golden brown. Transfer to the slow cooker.

2. Cook bacon in the same pan, turning occasionally, for 7-8 minutes until evenly browned. Transfer to the slow cooker.

3. Stir red wine, chicken stock, garlic, tarragon, thyme, bay leaf, salt and pepper into the slow cooker.

4. Cover and cook on low for 4 hours.

5. Add onion, carrots and mushrooms and cook for a further 45 minutes.

6. Remove bay leaf and serve with crusty bread on the side and garnished with extra tarragon and thyme leaves.

CAJUN CHICKEN WITH RICE

INGREDIENTS

3-4 chicken breasts, cut into bite-sized pieces

1 tbsp Cajun seasoning

¼ tsp cayenne pepper

½ tsp salt

¼ tsp pepper

Olive oil, for frying

3 cups (750ml, 24fl oz) chicken stock

1 onion, finely chopped

3 garlic cloves, finely minced

2 cups (310g, 8oz) short-grain rice

3 tomatoes, chopped

1 bay leaf

1 cup (170g, 6oz) frozen peas

1 tbsp thyme, chopped

6 bacon rashers

1 tbsp chives, chopped, to garnish

METHOD

1. Place the chicken in a bowl and add the Cajun seasoning, cayenne pepper, salt and pepper. Toss to cover the chicken with spices.

2. Heat oil in a large frying pan over medium-high heat. Add chicken and cook for 3 minutes each side, until golden brown. Remove chicken from pan and transfer to the slow cooker.

3. Deglaze the pan with a splash of stock and transfer liquid to the slow cooker.

4. Place onion, garlic, rice, stock, tomato, bay leaf, peas and thyme in the slow cooker and stir to combine.

5. Cover and cook on low for 6 hours or high for 4 hours.

6. Fry bacon in a frying pan over a medium-high heat for 3-5 minutes until crispy. Drain and chop into small pieces.

7. Remove bay leaf.

8. Serve rice topped with crispy bacon and chives.

HONEY BBQ CHICKEN TACOS

INGREDIENTS

½ cup (180g, 6oz) tomato sauce

¼ cup (90g, 3oz) honey

2 garlic cloves, finely minced

2 tbsps molasses

1 tbsp apple cider vinegar

1 tsp chilli powder

1 tsp paprika

½ tsp salt

¼ tsp pepper

4 chicken breasts

120g (4oz) cream cheese, cubed

1 cup (125g, 4oz) Cheddar cheese, grated

½ cup (20g, ¾ oz) coriander, chopped

METHOD

1. In a medium mixing bowl, combine the tomato sauce, honey, garlic, molasses, apple cider vinegar, chilli powder, paprika, salt and pepper and stir well to combine.

2. Place chicken breasts in bottom of slow cooker. Pour sauce over the top of the chicken.

3. Cover and cook on low for 3½ hours or high for 2 hours.

4. Remove chicken from the slow cooker and set aside until cool enough to handle.

5. Scrape the sauce out of the slow cooker and place in a large bowl. Add cream cheese, Cheddar and coriander to the bowl and set aside.

6. Shred the chicken using two forks.

7. Transfer shredded chicken to the bowl and mix to combine.

8. Serve on soft tacos with desired garnish.

CHICKEN STROGANOFF

INGREDIENTS

1 onion, sliced

1 garlic clove, minced

225g (8oz) mushrooms, sliced

4 chicken breasts, cut into bite-sized slices

½ tsp salt

¼ tsp pepper

1 cup (250ml, 8fl oz) chicken stock

1 tsp Dijon mustard

¼ cup (60ml, 2fl oz) dry white wine

3 tbsps plain flour

1 bay leaf

420g (15oz) wide tagliatelli

¼ cup (50g, 2oz) sour cream

Parsley, chopped, for garnish

METHOD

1. Combine onion, garlic, mushrooms, chicken, salt and pepper in a medium slow cooker. Stir to combine. Set aside.

2. Place chicken stock, mustard, wine and flour in a medium bowl and whisk until thoroughly incorporated.

3. Pour stock mixture over chicken in the slow cooker. Add bay leaf.

4. Cover and cook on low for 4½ hours or high for 2½ hours, until chicken is cooked through.

5. Cook the pasta according to the instructions on the packet.

6. Before serving, remove bay leaf, stir in sour cream and garnish with fresh parsley. Serve with pasta.

APRICOT CHICKEN

INGREDIENTS

¼ cup (30g, 1oz) slivered almonds

1 tsp olive oil

1kg (2lb) boneless, skinless chicken thighs

1 tsp paprika

½ tsp salt

¼ tsp pepper

1 cup (250ml, 8fl oz) chicken stock

1 lemon, zested and juiced

3 tbsps Dijon mustard

4 garlic cloves, minced

1 tsp dried thyme

1 cup (150g, 5oz) onion, sliced

1 cup (190g, 7oz) dried apricots, halved if desired

METHOD

1. Heat a large frying pan over medium-high heat. Dry fry the slivered almonds for 3 minutes or until they start to brown. Remove them immediately from the heat and set aside.

2. Heat the olive oil over medium-high heat.

3. Season chicken thighs with paprika, salt and pepper. Add to pan and cook for 5-6 minutes, until browned, turning once.

4. Combine chicken stock, lemon zest and juice, mustard, garlic and thyme in the slow cooker and whisk to combine. (Or you can stir it all together in a small bowl and add to your slow cooker.)

5. Add onions, apricots and seared chicken thighs to the slow cooker.

6. Cover and cook on low for 6-8 hours or high for 3-4 hours.

7. Serve chicken thighs and plenty of sauce over whole wheat couscous or brown rice.

8. Garnish with slivered almonds.

CHICKEN AND MUSHROOM POT PIES

INGREDIENTS

4 carrots, diced

1 onion, chopped

⅓ cup (40g, 1½oz) plain flour

2 sprigs fresh thyme

1 bay leaf

½ cup (125ml, 4fl oz) chicken stock (or water)

8 skinless chicken thighs

½ tsp salt

¼ tsp pepper

1 cup (170g, 6oz) frozen peas

225g (8oz, ½ lb) button mushrooms, quartered

⅓ cup (80ml, 3fl oz) thickened cream

1-2 sheets puff pastry, thawed

1 egg, beaten

METHOD

1. Combine the carrots, onion, flour, thyme, bay leaf and stock in a medium slow cooker. Place the chicken on top and season with salt and pepper.

2. Cover and cook on low for 7 hours or on high for 4 hours.

3. Thirty minutes before serving, preheat the oven to 200°C (400°F, Gas Mark 6).

4. Remove chicken from the slow cooker and set aside until cool enough to handle. Shred the chicken using two forks and return to the slow cooker.

5. Add the peas, mushrooms and cream to the chicken mixture and stir to combine. Cover and cook on high or low for 5 minutes until heated through.

6. Divide the filling between four ramekins or small baking dishes.

7. Cut eight circles slightly bigger than the dishes from the puff pastry and top each pie with two pastry circles. Lightly brush with egg. Place on a baking tray and bake for 10 minutes or until the pastry is puffed up and golden.

MOROCCAN LEMON CHICKEN

INGREDIENTS

6 saffron threads

2½ cups (600ml, 21fl oz) chicken stock, hot

2 tbsps olive oil

8 chicken pieces (leg, thigh and breast)

1 large onion, chopped

3 garlic cloves, finely chopped

1 tsp ground ginger

1 tsp ground coriander

1 cinnamon stick

16 green olives

1 red chilli, finely diced (optional)

½ cup (20g, ¾ oz) coriander, leaves picked (retaining some for garnish)

1 large lemon, thinly sliced

METHOD

1. Soak the saffron in the jug of hot stock. Set aside.

2. Heat oil in a large frying pan over medium-high heat. Add chicken and cook for 3 minutes each side, until golden brown. Transfer to the slow cooker.

3. Add the onion to the frying pan and reduce heat to medium-low. Cook for 5 minutes until soft. Transfer to the slow cooker.

4. Place the garlic, ginger, coriander, cinammon stick and saffron threads and stock into the slow cooker.

5. Cover and cook on low for 8 hours or on high for 4 hours.

6. Thirty minutes before serving, add olives, chilli (if using) and coriander to the slow cooker. Arrange the lemon slices over the top.

7. Serve garnished with retained coriander.

CHICKEN TAQUITOS

INGREDIENTS

2 large chicken breasts

1 tsp chilli powder

1 garlic clove, finely minced

2 tsps cumin

2 tsps ground oregano

½ tsp salt

¼ tsp pepper

225g (8oz, ½ lb) cream cheese, cubed

1 cup (125g, 4oz) Cheddar cheese, grated

⅓ cup (80ml, 3fl oz) water

12 mini tortillas

¼ cup (25g, 1oz) spring onion, chopped, to garnish

METHOD

1. Place chicken, chilli powder, garlic, cumin, oregano, salt and pepper, cream cheese, half the Cheddar cheese and water into slow cooker.

2. Cover and cook on low for 8 hours or on high for 4 hours.

3. Thirty minutes before serving, remove chicken from slow cooker. Shred with two forks, and return chicken to slow cooker. Stir and cook for a further 15 minutes.

4. Preheat oven to 200°C (400°F, Gas Mark 6).

5. Place a heaped tablespoon of chicken mixture onto the middle of each tortilla. Top with grated cheese. Roll tightly and place in a single layer on a lined baking tray.

6. Transfer to the oven and bake for 10 minutes, until cheese has melted slightly.

7. Serve garnished with spring onion.

SERVES 2 ★ PREP 10MIN ★ COOK TIME 8HR LOW

PAPRIKA CHICKEN

METHOD

1. Combine flour and chicken in a medium bowl and toss well to coat.

2. Heat oil in a large frying pan over medium-high. Add chicken and cook for 3 minutes each side, until golden brown. Transfer to the slow cooker.

3. Place chicken, onion, stock, capsicum, carrot, paprika, garlic, salt, pepper and mushrooms into the slow cooker.

4. Cover and cook on low for 8 hours.

5. Stir in sour cream.

6. Serve garnished with extra paprika.

INGREDIENTS

1 tbsp plain flour

2 small chicken breasts

Olive oil, for frying

1 small onion, chopped

1 cup (250ml, 8fl oz) chicken stock

½ green capsicum, seeded and finely sliced

1 carrot, diced

2 tbsps Hungarian sweet paprika

2 garlic cloves, minced

1 tsp salt

1 tsp pepper

150g (5oz) mushrooms, sliced

¾ cup (185ml, 6fl oz) sour cream

Paprika, to garnish

RED CHICKEN CURRY

INGREDIENTS

4 chicken breasts

1 x 400ml (14fl oz) can coconut milk

¼ cup (65g, 2oz) peanut butter

2 tbsps red curry paste

2 tbsps fish sauce

3 tbsps lime juice

2 tbsps brown sugar

4 garlic cloves, minced

2 lemongrass stalks, white part finely chopped

1 cup (250ml, 8fl oz) chicken stock

Medium piece ginger, minced

1-2 small red chillies, sliced (optional)

1 cup (170g, 6oz) frozen peas

6 Thai eggplants, quartered

Basil leaves, to garnish

METHOD

1. Place chicken in the bottom of the slow cooker.

2. Combine coconut milk, peanut butter, red curry paste, fish sauce, lime juice, brown sugar, garlic, lemongrass, chicken stock and ginger in a large bowl.

3. Pour sauce into the slow cooker. Add chillies, if using, as well as the peas and eggplant.

4. Cover and cook on low for 3 hours.

5. Remove chicken from the slow cooker and cut into large pieces. Return to the sauce to keep warm.

6. Serve garnished with fresh basil.

CHICKEN WITH TOMATOES AND HERBS

INGREDIENTS

30g (1oz) butter

8 chicken pieces

4 small onions, chopped

8 Roma tomatoes, chopped

3 garlic cloves, minced

¾ cup (25g, 1oz) parsley leaves, roughly chopped

¾ cup (25g, 1oz) coriander leaves, roughly chopped

¾ cup (25g, 1oz) basil

¾ cup (25g, 1oz) dill

½ cup (125ml, 4fl oz) chicken stock

1 tbsp lemon juice

½ tsp chilli flakes

1 tsp salt

½ tsp pepper

Lemon slices, to garnish

METHOD

1. Heat the butter in a large frying pan over medium-high heat. Add chicken and cook for 4 minutes each side, until golden brown. Transfer to the slow cooker.

2. Add the chopped onions to the frying pan and reduce heat to medium-low. Cook for 10 minutes until very soft. Transfer to the slow cooker.

3. Add the tomatoes, garlic, parsley, coriander, basil, dill, stock, lemon juice, chilli flakes, salt and pepper to the slow cooker. Retain some herbs for garnish.

4. Cover and cook on high for 2 hours.

5. Serve garnished with extra fresh herbs and lemon slices.

CHICKEN DRUMSTICKS WITH CAPSICUM

INGREDIENTS

6-8 chicken drumsticks

1 tbsp plain flour

Salt and pepper, to taste

2 tbsps canola oil

2 small red capsicums, seeded and thickly sliced

1 small yellow capsicum, thickly sliced

8 shallots, peeled

6 small garlic cloves, smashed

1 x 400g (14oz) can diced tomatoes

1 tsp Dijon mustard

¼ cup (60ml, 2fl oz) white wine vinegar

1 cup (250ml, 8fl oz) chicken stock

METHOD

1. Pat chicken dry with paper towels. Dust the tops with a light coating of flour and season with salt and pepper.

2. Heat the oil in a large frying pan over medium-high heat. Add drumsticks in batches and cook for 2 minutes each side, until lightly browned. Transfer to the slow cooker.

3. Add the capsicums, shallots, garlic, tomatoes, mustard, vinegar, stock and a couple of good grinds of salt and pepper to the slow cooker.

4. Cover and cook on high for 2 hours.

5. Season to taste and serve hot.

GLAZED DUCK WITH FIGS

INGREDIENTS

2 duck Marylands

1 tbsp rosemary, finely chopped

1 tsp salt

1 tsp pepper

1 red onion, peeled and finely chopped

2 fresh figs, quartered

½ cup (125ml, 4fl oz) red wine

1 cup (250ml, 8fl oz) chicken stock

1 bay leaf

3-4 small sprigs of fresh rosemary

10 sprigs of thyme, leaves picked

METHOD

1. Trim the duck legs of as much excess fat as you can then pat them dry and rub with chopped rosemary, salt and pepper.

2. Heat a large frying pan over medium-high heat and add the duck breasts, flat side down. Cook for 3 minutes each side until golden and the fat runs out freely. Transfer to the slow cooker and place skin side up.

3. Place the onion and 4 fig quarters around the duck, then pour the fat from the pan over the duck and onions.

4. Pour the red wine and stock around the legs and add the bay leaf.

5. Cook in the slow cooker on low for 6 hours.

6. Half an hour before the end of cooking, add the remaining fig quarters and the sprigs of rosemary and thyme.

7. Season and then serve with mashed potatoes and vegetables of your choice.

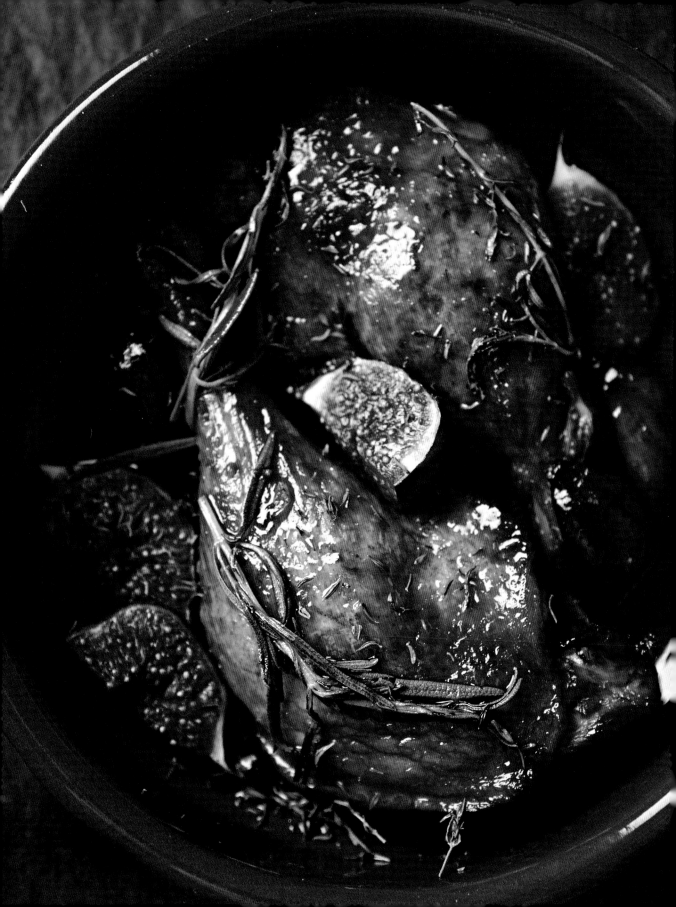

CHICKEN TIKKA MASALA

INGREDIENTS

8 boneless, skinless chicken thighs, cut into bite-sized pieces

¾ cup (185ml, 6fl oz) plain yoghurt

1 onion, diced

3 garlic cloves, minced

Small piece fresh ginger, minced

2 tbsps tomato paste

1 tbsp garam masala

2 tsps smoked paprika

2 tsps salt

2 x 400g (14oz) cans diced tomatoes

¾ cup (185ml, 6fl oz) coconut milk

Parsley, chopped, to garnish

METHOD

1. Place chicken and yoghurt in a medium bowl and toss to combine. Cover with plastic wrap and transfer to the fridge to marinate for at least 1 hour..

2. Shake or wipe chicken to remove excess yogurt before transferring to the slow cooker.

3. Stir in the onion, garlic, ginger, tomato paste, garam masala, paprika and salt until the chicken is evenly covered with spices. Stir in the diced tomatoes.

4. Cover and cook for 8 hours on low or 4 hours on high.

5. If you prefer a thicker sauce, leave the slow cooker uncovered for the last 15 minutes

6. Just before the end of cooking, stir in the coconut milk.

HOMEMADE CHICKEN STOCK

INGREDIENTS

1 whole chicken carcass

2 tbsps apple cider vinegar

8 cups (2L, 4pt) water

1 onion, quartered

2 carrots, peeled and quartered

1 celery stalk, roughly chopped

2 bay leaves

8 peppercorns

1 tbsp salt

1 bunch parsley (optional)

METHOD

1. Combine all the ingredients, except parsley, in a large slow cooker.

2. Cover and cook on low for 24 hours. Fifteen minutes before finishing the stock, add parsley (if using).

3. Turn off slow cooker and skim off any particles that have floated to the top.

4. Allow to cool, then strain. Retain liquid and discard vegetables and chicken carcass.

5. Refrigerate and use when needed (or freeze for up to 3 months).

CHICKEN WITH RICE AND SULTANAS

INGREDIENTS

6 cups (1.5L, 50fl oz) water

3 tsps salt

2 cups (310g, 8oz) basmati rice, rinsed

4 saffron threads

3 tbsps hot water

2 large onions

4 tbsps ghee (or olive oil)

Medium piece fresh ginger, peeled and chopped

8 garlic cloves, coarsely chopped

1 medium tomato, quartered

1 tbsp plain yoghurt

2 tbsps garam masala

1 tbsp ground coriander

1 tsp cayenne pepper

12 mixed chicken pieces

¼ cup (30g, 1oz) cashews

½ cup (70g, 2½ oz) olives

½ cup (80g, 3oz) sultanas

½ cup (125ml, 4fl oz) chicken stock

¼ cup (10g, ¼ oz) parsley, chopped

METHOD

1. Boil the water with 1 teaspoon salt in a large saucepan. Stir in the rice and cook for 6 minutes. Rinse in cold water and leave to drain.

2. Add the saffron threads to the hot water in a small bowl. Set aside.

3. Halve and slice 1 onion and roughly chop the other. In a large frying pan, heat 3 tablespoons of the ghee over high heat and fry the sliced onion for 8 minutes, stirring constantly, until dark brown and crisp. Leaving as much of the ghee as possible in the pan, transfer the onion with a slotted spoon to a plate lined with paper towel and set aside.

4. Add the chopped onion to the same pan and saute over medium-high heat for 5 minutes until lightly browned. Transfer the onion to a food processor. Add the ginger, garlic and tomato and process into a paste. Add the yoghurt, along with the garam masala, coriander, cayenne pepper and the rest of the salt and process for 1 more minute. Pour the puree over the chicken pieces in a large bowl and coat the pieces. Let sit for 30 minutes.

5. Heat the slow cooker on high for 15 minutes before use. Melt the rest of the ghee in the cooker. Layer the chicken pieces in the cooker, then stir in the rice as well as the saffron liquid and strands, the cashews, olives, sultanas and fried onion slices. Pour the stock over the top.

6. Cover the inset of the slow cooker with aluminum foil, and fold the foil over the sides of the slow cooker. Place the lid on the cooker and cook on low for 4 hours.

7. Remove the inset from the cooker and let it stand for about 5 minutes. Season to taste and serve hot garnished with parsley

SWEET AND SOUR CHICKEN

INGREDIENTS

3 tbsps sesame seeds

1 tbsp canola oil

700g (1½ lb) chicken fillets, cut into bite-size chunks

1 red capsicum, seeded and thickly sliced

1 x 225g (8oz) can diced pineapple in juice

2 cups (500ml, 1pt) chicken stock

¼ cup (60ml, 2fl oz) apple cider vinegar

3 tbsps light brown sugar

2 small garlic cloves, crushed

2 tsps tamari sauce (or light soy sauce)

3 tbsps arrowroot flour

¼ cup (60ml, 2fl oz) cold water

METHOD

1. Heat a small frying pan over medium-high heat. Dry fry the sesame seeds for 2 minutes or until they start to brown. Remove them immediately from the pan and set aside.

2. Pour the oil in the slow cooker and stir the chicken pieces around to coat. Add capsicum and pineapple chunks to the slow cooker, retaining the pinepple juice for use in the next step.

3. In a small saucepan, combine ⅓ cup pineapple juicen, vinegar, brown sugar, garlic and tamari. Heat over medium heat and stir until the sugar dissolves. Pour the sauce over the chicken in the slow cooker.

4. Cover the cooker and cook on low for 8 hours.

5. In a small bowl or glass, vigorously stir the flour and water together, then pour into the cooker and stir through until the sauce has thickened.

6. Cook for 30 more minutes on low.

7. Serve the chicken warm with the sauce and garnished with sesame seeds.

CHICKEN TERIYAKI

INGREDIENTS

2 tbsps sesame seeds

4 skinless chicken breasts

¾ cup (185ml, 6fl oz) tamari or light soy sauce

½ cup (180g, 6oz) honey

½ cup (125ml, 4fl oz) rice wine vinegar

2 tbsps mirin

2 tsps sesame oil

4 large garlic cloves, crushed

1½ tbsps fresh ginger, minced

3 tbsps arrowroot flour

⅓ cup (80ml, 3fl oz) cold water

3 cups (495g, 1lb 1oz) cooked white rice

3 cups (495g, 1lb 1oz) steamed broccoli florets

3 tbsps chives, chopped

1 small red chilli, seeded and thinly sliced

METHOD

1. Heat a small frying pan over medium-high heat. Dry fry the sesame seeds for 3 minutes or until they start to brown. Remove the seeds immediately from the heat and set aside.

2. Place the chicken in the slow cooker. In a small bowl, whisk together the tamari, honey, vinegar, mirin, sesame oil, garlic and ginger and pour over chicken. Cover and cook on low for 3-4 hours or high for 2-3 hours.

3. In a small glass, vigorously stir together the arrowroot flour with water and pour into the slow cooker and stir through. Cook on high for another 30-40 minutes, or until sauce has thickened. . Remove the chicken breasts and thickly slice.

4. Serve the sliced chicken on a bed of rice with steamed broccoli on the side.

5. Drizzle with leftover sauce from the slow cooker and garnish with chives, chilli and sesame seeds.

MAPLE DIJON CHICKEN

INGREDIENTS

4 medium chicken breasts, cut into bite-size chunks

8 tsps brown sugar

Salt and pepper, to taste

2 tbsps olive oil

2 tbsps fresh basil leaves, to garnish

Sauce

⅓ cup (105g, 4oz) maple syrup

3 tbsps Dijon mustard

1 tbsp whole grain mustard

1 tbsp balsamic vinegar

3 small garlic cloves, crushed

1 tsp ground oregano

3 tbsps orange juice

Salt and pepper, to taste

METHOD

1. In a medium bowl, whisk together maple syrup, mustards, vinegar, garlic, oregano and orange juice; season with salt and pepper, to taste. Set aside.

2. Toss the chicken pieces with the sugar and a couple of good grinds of salt and pepper in a large mixing bowl.

3. Heat the oil in a large frying pan over medium-high heat. Fry the chicken for 4 minutes, turning halfway, until golden brown.

4. Place the chicken pieces in the slow cooker and pour over the maple Dijon mixture.

5. Cover and cook on low heat for 3 hours.

6. Season to taste and serve warm garnished with basil leaves.

FARMHOUSE CHICKEN BROTH WITH DUMPLINGS

INGREDIENTS

1 tbsp oil

1 small leek, sliced

1 onion, diced

1 large potato, peeled and cut into 1cm (½ in) cubes

2 small carrots, chopped

6 cups (1.5L, 50fl oz) chicken stock

¼ cup (10g, ¼ oz) flat-leaf parsley, roughly chopped

Salt and pepper, to taste

Dumplings

1 cup (125g, 4oz) plain flour

2 tsps baking powder

1 tsp caster sugar

½ tsp salt

1 tbsp butter

½ cup (125ml, 4fl oz) whole milk

METHOD

1. Heat the oil in a large saucepan over medium-high heat. Add the leek and onion and fry for 5 minutes until softened and browned. Add the potato and carrot and cook for another 3 minutes.

2. Add the vegetables to the slow cooker with the stock. Cover and cook on low for 7½ hours.

3. Turn the heat up to high, then mix the dumpling ingredients together in the order listed. The dough will be sticky.

4. Drop the dough in large spoonfuls into the slow cooker. They will stick briefly to each other at first, but they will separate as they cook.

5. Cook for another hour. Season to taste.

6. Serve garnished with parsley.

VEGETABLES

Spanish tortilla	114
Healthy lentil casserole	116
Vegetable barley nourishing bowls	117
Pumpkin Risotto	118
Slow roast potatoes with dill	120
Quinoa with vegetables	121
Bean and vegetable enchiladas	122
Marsala mushrooms	124
Cabbage rolls	125
Barley risotto with mushroom and pumpkin	126
Honey glazed carrots	128
Homestyle tomato sauce	129
Pumpkin soup with roasted hazelnuts	130
Minestrone soup	132
Creamy cheesy pasta	133
Russian borscht	134
Moroccan stew	136
Stuffed capsicum	137
Roast garlic and tomato soup	138
Lentil tamarind soup	140
Mexican corn	141
Loaded potato skins	142
White bean soup	144
Spicy ratatouille	145
Moroccan harira soup	146
Coconut soup with quinoa and vegetables	148
Vegetable stew	149
Homestyle beans	150
Spiced pumpkin and chickpea stew	152
Wild rice and mushrooms	153
Soft polenta	154

SPANISH TORTILLA

INGREDIENTS

2 cups (150g, 5oz) small broccoli florets

Olive oil, for frying

1 onion, chopped

3 medium potatoes, peeled and diced

3 eggs

6 egg whites

2 tbsps capers

¼ tsp salt

¼ tsp pepper

¼ cup (30g, 1oz) Parmesan cheese, grated

¼ cup (10g, ¼oz) parsley leaves, to garnish

METHOD

1. Steam the broccoli florets for 10 minutes until soft. Use a masher to break them down. Set aside and let cool.

2. Heat the oil in a large frying pan over medium-high heat. Add onion and potato and cook, stirring occasionally, for 6-8 minutes until onion is soft and potato is golden brown.

3. Lightly grease a medium slow cooker with oil. Place potato and onion mixture in the base.

4. Combine eggs, egg whites, capers, salt and pepper with the broccoli in a medium bowl and whisk to combine.

5. Pour egg mixture over potatoes and onions in slow cooker. Sprinkle over the Parmesan cheese.

6. Cover and cook on low for 2½ hours.

7. Turn off the slow cooker and allow to stand, covered, for 10 minutes.

8. Serve garnished with parsley leaves.

HEALTHY LENTIL CASSEROLE

INGREDIENTS

2 cups (370g, 12oz) red (or yellow) lentils, rinsed

1 cup (250ml, 8fl oz) vegetable stock

1 small onion, diced

1 celery stalk, diced into small pieces

2 x 400g (14oz) cans diced tomatoes, drained

1 x 400g (14oz) can chickpeas, rinsed and drained

3 garlic cloves, minced

1 bay leaf

¼ tsp salt

¼ tsp pepper

⅛ tsp turmeric

¼ tsp ground cumin

¼ tsp ground coriander

¼ tsp chilli flakes

¼ tsp cayenne pepper

Parsley, chopped, to garnish

Lemon wedges, to serve

METHOD

1. Rinse the lentils 2-3 times under running water.

2. Place all the ingredients except garnishes into the slow cooker, turn on low and cook for 5-6 hours.

3. Garnish with fresh parsley and lemon wedges, and serve on its own or with rice.

VEGETABLE BARLEY NOURISHING BOWLS

INGREDIENTS

2 tbsps olive oil

2 small onions, chopped

1 cup (100g, 3½ oz) celery, finely chopped

3 small garlic cloves, crushed

4 medium carrots, cut into 4cm (1½ in) long strips

2 large Desiree potatoes, peeled and cut into 1cm (½ in) cubes

8 cups (2L, 4pt) vegetable stock

1 cup (200g, 7oz) pearl barley, rinsed

1 large zucchini, quartered and sliced

1 punnet cherry tomatoes, halved

200g (7oz) shiitake mushrooms, sliced

Salt and pepper, to taste

¼ cup (10g, ¼ oz) flat-leaf parsley, roughly chopped

METHOD

1. Heat the oil in a large frying pan over medium-high heat. Add the onion and celery and fry for 3 minutes until softened and browned. Add the garlic, carrots and potatoes and fry for another 3 minutes.

2. Turn the slow cooker on to low and add the cooked vegetables.

3. Pour over the stock and add the barley, zucchini, tomatoes, mushrooms and a couple of good grinds of salt and pepper.

4. Cover and cook on low for 4 hours.

5. Season to taste and serve garnished with parsley

PUMPKIN RISOTTO

INGREDIENTS

1 small butternut pumpkin, peeled, seeded and diced

3 tbsps olive oil

Salt and pepper, to taste

2 tsps dried sage

½ cup (75g, 3oz) chopped onion

1 tbsp crushed garlic

1½ cups (235g, 7oz) Arborio rice

4 cups (1L, 2pt) vegetable stock (or water)

2 tsps salt

1 tsp pepper

½ cup (10g, ¼ oz) fresh sage leaves, to garnish

METHOD

1. Preheat the oven to 180°C (350°F, Gas Mark 4).

2. Drizzle the pumpkin with 2 tablespoons olive oil and sprinkle with salt, pepper and sage. Transfer to the oven to roast for 45 minutes until soft. Remove from the oven and set aside to cool slightly.

3. Transfer half of the pumpkin to a blender and pulse until a puree forms. Set aside. (This will give your risotto a rich orange colour, but you can omit this step and simply add all the pumpkin pieces in step 6 below, if you like).

4. Heat 1 tablespoon olive oil in a medium frying pan over a medium-high heat. Add the onion and cook, stirring occasionally, until softened, about 4-5 minutes. Add the garlic and cook for a further 1 minute, until fragrant. Stir in the Arborio rice and cook for an additional 2-3 minutes.

5. Transfer the rice and onion mixture to a lightly greased slow cooker. Stir in the vegetable stock, salt, pepper and pumpkin puree.

6. Cover the slow cooker and cook on high for 1½ hours, until the rice is tender. Stir in the retained roast pumpkin pieces. Add salt and pepper, to taste, before serving garnished with fresh sage.

SLOW ROAST POTATOES WITH DILL

INGREDIENTS

800g (1¾ lb) roasting potatoes, (Nicola or pontiac)

¼ cup (60ml, 2fl oz) duck fat, melted

300g (10oz) mushrooms, thickly sliced

4 small garlic cloves, crushed

1 tbsp salt

1 tsp pepper

2 tsps onion powder

½ tsp cayenne pepper

¼ cup (10g, ¼ oz) dill, finely chopped

METHOD

1. Peel the potatoes and cut into 1cm (½ in) thick slices.

2. Toss the melted duck fat in a large bowl together with the potatoes, mushrooms, garlic, salt, pepper, onion powder and cayenne. Ensure the potatoes and mushrooms are thoroughly coated.

3. Place the potatoes and mushrooms in the slow cooker and drizzle over any remaining melted fat. Spread everything out as evenly as possible.

4. Cover and cook on high for 3 hours until the potatoes are tender when pierced with a knife.

5. Serve immediately, garnished with dill.

QUINOA WITH VEGETABLES

INGREDIENTS

1½ cups (340g, 12oz) quinoa

1 tbsp olive oil

3 cups (750ml, 24fl oz) chicken or vegetable stock

1 large onion, chopped

1 medium red capsicum, finely chopped

1 small yellow capsicum, finely chopped

1 small green capsicum, finely chopped

2 cups (630g, 1lb 6oz) cauliflower, chopped

1 small zucchini, chopped

2 garlic cloves, crushed

¼ tsp pepper

Sprigs of parsley, to garnish

METHOD

1. Rinse quinoa and add to the cooker.

2. Stir through 1 tablespoon of olive oil to coat.

3. Stir in stock, veggies, garlic and pepper.

4. Cover and cook on low for 4-6 hours, or on high for 2-4.

5. The quinoa is done when you can fluff it with a fork and it is tender. All the liquid should be absorbed.

6. Garnish with parsley and serve.

   Note: You can mix in chickpeas or black beans to add protein to this dish and turn it into a meal.

BEAN AND VEGETABLE ENCHILADAS

INGREDIENTS

2 cups (550g, 1¼ lb) salsa, divided

1 cup (225g, 8oz) tomato passata

1 x 400g (14oz) can kidney beans, rinsed and drained

1 cup (175g, 6oz) fresh corn kernels

1 large yellow capsicum, finely diced

1 small onion, chopped

Salt and pepper, to taste

¼ cup (20g, ¾ oz) jalapenos, finely chopped

Cooking spray

8 medium (15cm/6in) corn tortillas

1½ cups (185g, 6oz) Edam or Cheddar cheese, grated

METHOD

1. Use a blender or stick blender to puree 1½ cups salsa and the passata sauce together into a smooth enchilada sauce.

2. Combine beans, corn, capsicum, onion, remaining ½ cup salsa and ½ cup of the enchilada sauce as well as a couple of good grinds of salt and pepper in a large bowl.

3. In a separate bowl, combine remaining enchilada sauce and jalapenos.

4. Spray the inside of your slow cooker with cooking spray. Spread ¼ cup of the sauce over the bottom of the cooker.

5. Divide the bean and vegetable mixture between the tortillas, placing along the centre of each, then roll each tortilla up and place them next to each other snugly in the cooker, seam side down. Top with the remaining sauce and cheese. Ideally they'll be in one layer, but if not, top each layer with half the sauce and half the cheese.

6. Cook on low 3 hours.

MARSALA MUSHROOMS

INGREDIENTS

1 tbsp butter

4 rashers bacon, finely chopped

1 tsp maple syrup

700g (1½ lb) Swiss or button mushrooms, cleaned, trimmed and halved

⅓ cup (50g, 2oz) diced shallot

2 garlic cloves, finely chopped

2 tbsps fresh parsley, chopped

¼ cup (60ml, 2fl oz) sweet Marsala

¼ cup (60ml, 2fl oz) chicken stock

Salt and pepper, to taste

½ cup (125ml, 4fl oz) thickened cream

1 tsp cornflour

Parmesan cheese, grated

2 tbsps chives, chopped

METHOD

1. Heat the butter in a small frying pan over medium-high heat. Add the bacon and maple syrup and fry for 8 minutes until crispy. Remove from the pan and drain on paper towels.

2. Lightly butter the slow cooker. Arrange mushrooms across bottom – it's okay if there is overlap; the mushrooms will shrink considerably as they cook. Sprinkle with shallots, garlic and parsley.

3. In small bowl, mix Marsala and chicken stock; pour over mushrooms. Sprinkle with salt and pepper.

4. Cover and cook on low for 8 hours. About 30 to 60 minutes before end of cook time, in small bowl, stir thickened cream with cornflour to dissolve. Gently stir mixture into liquid in slow cooker for remaining cook time. Taste for seasoning; add salt if needed.

5. Serve with a sprinkle of Parmesan, bacon and chives.

SERVES 4 ★ PREP 40min ★ COOK TIME 8hr LOW

CABBAGE ROLLS

INGREDIENTS

12 large savoy cabbage leaves

1 large egg, beaten

1 cup (225g, 8oz) plus ¼ cup (60g, 2oz) tomato passata

½ small onion, finely chopped

1 tsp salt

¼ tsp pepper

1kg (2lb) lean minced beef

1 cup (165g, 6oz) cooked rice

¼ cup (60ml, 2fl oz) vegetable stock

1 tbsp brown sugar

1 tbsp lemon juice

1 tsp Worcestershire sauce

⅓ cup (15g, ½ oz) fresh parsley, finely chopped

1 cup (250ml, 8fl oz) sour cream (or Greek yoghurt)

METHOD

1. Prepare a large bowl of boiling water. Immerse cabbage leaves in water for about 3 minutes or until limp. Drain and set aside.

2. Combine egg, ¼ cup of passata, onion, salt, pepper, beef, and cooked rice.

3. Place about ¼ cup of the meat mixture in the centre of each cabbage leaf. Tuck in each short end and roll lenthwise, placing seam side down on the inset of your slow cooker.

4. Combine the 1 cup passata, stock, brown sugar, lemon juice and Worcestershire sauce in a small mixing bowl and whisk to combine. Pour the mixture over the cabbage rolls.

5. Cover and cook on low for 7-9 hours.

6. Serve warm garnished with parsley and sour cream.

BARLEY RISOTTO WITH MUSHROOM AND PUMPKIN

INGREDIENTS

5 tbsps unsalted butter

2 tbsps olive oil

½ cup (50g, 2oz) spring onion, finely chopped

1½ cups (300g, 10oz) pearl barley

1 tsp salt

½ tsp pepper

¼ cup (60ml, 2fl oz) dry white wine (or water)

350g (12oz) button mushrooms

350g (12oz) butternut pumpkin, diced

½ cup (50g, 2oz) carrot, grated

4 cups (1L, 2pt) chicken stock

1 cup (100g, 3½ oz) Parmesan cheese, finely grated

¼ cup (10g, ¼ oz) fresh dill, finely chopped

METHOD

1. Heat 1 tablespoon butter and 1 tablespoon oil in a large deep-sided frying pan over medium-high heat. Add the spring onions and cook, stirring, for 2-3 minutes or until tender but not brown. Add the barley, salt and pepper and cook for a further 1 minute. Pour in the white wine (or water) and cook, stirring for 1 to 2 minutes, until evaporated. Transfer the barley mixture to a large slow cooker.

2. Add 2 tablespoons butter and the remaining 1 tablespoon oil to the same pan over medium-high heat. Add the mushrooms and cook for 5 minutes, until just browned and softened. Add the mushrooms, pumpkin, carrot and stock to the slow cooker. Stir gently to combine.

3. Set the slow cooker to low and cook for 2-3 hours until the liquid is absorbed and the barley and pumpkin are tender. Remove the lid and stir in half of the cheese and the remaining 2 tablespoons butter. Season to taste.

4. Serve hot, garnished with the remaining cheese and dill.

HONEY GLAZED CARROTS

INGREDIENTS

½ cup (60g, 2oz) walnuts, roughly chopped

Cooking spray

16 baby carrots

¼ cup (90g, 3oz) honey

½ tsp salt

¼ cup (40g, 1½ oz) packed brown sugar

2 tbsps butter, melted

¼ cup (60ml, 2fl oz) vegetable stock

METHOD

1. Heat a small frying pan over medium-high heat. Dry fry the walnuts for 3 minutes or until they start to brown. Remove walnuts immediately from the pan and set aside.

2. Spray the slow cooker with cooking spray. Add the carrots. Mix together the honey, salt, sugar, butter and stock and drizzle over the carrots.

3. Cover; cook on high heat setting 4 to 5 hours, stirring after 2 hours, or until carrots are desired tenderness.

4. Spoon carrots into a serving bowl; spoon any sauce from the slow cooker over them.

5. Garnish with the toasted walnuts.

HOMESTYLE TOMATO SAUCE

1.5kg (3lb 5oz) vine-ripened tomatoes, chopped

½ onion, roughly chopped

¼ cup (10g, ¼ oz) flat-leaf parsley, chopped

10 basil leaves

2-3 garlic cloves, minced

½ tsp thyme

1 tsp brown sugar

1 tsp oregano

Salt and pepper, to taste

1. Place all the ingredients in a slow cooker and cook on high for 5 hours. (Cooking for longer allows the flavours to further develop.)

Note: To thicken the sauce, cook uncovered for the final hour of cooking. For a smooth sauce, puree with a stick blender.

PUMPKIN SOUP WITH ROASTED HAZELNUTS

INGREDIENTS

1kg (2lb) pumpkin, chopped

1-2 onions, chopped

2 cups (500ml, 1pt) chicken (or vegetable) stock

1 cup (125g, 4oz) hazelnuts

½ cup (125ml, 4fl oz) thickened cream (or sour cream)

Pinch of nutmeg

Salt and pepper, to taste

Fresh parsley, to garnish

METHOD

1. Place the pumpkin, onion and stock in a medium slow cooker.

2. Cover and cook on low for 7 hours until pumpkin is soft.

3. Preheat the oven to 150°C (300°F, Gas Mark 2).

4. Spread hazelnuts in an even layer on a baking tray and transfer to the oven. Bake for 10-15 minutes until deep brown and aromatic. Be careful not to burn. Remove from oven and set aside to cool slightly.

5. Using a clean tea towel rub hazelnuts to loosen and shed skins. Roughly chop and set aside.

6. Blend cooked soup in the slow cooker with a stick blender or in batches with a stand blender.

7. Stir in cream and nutmeg. Season to taste.

8. Serve garnished with roasted hazelnuts and fresh parsley.

MINESTRONE SOUP

INGREDIENTS

3 cups (750ml, 24fl oz) vegetable or chicken stock

2 x 400g (14oz) cans diced tomatoes

1 x 400g (14oz) can kidney beans, drained

2 carrots, peeled and chopped

1 celery stalk, chopped

1 onion, chopped

½ bunch thyme, leaves picked and chopped

2 bay leaves

½ tsp salt

½ tsp pepper

275g (10oz) cooked ditalini (or macaroni) pasta

1 bunch spinach, leaves picked and chopped

Micro greens, to garnish (optional)

METHOD

1. Place stock, tomatoes, beans, carrots, celery, onion, thyme, bay leaves, salt and black pepper into a medium slow cooker.

2. Cover and cook on low for 6 hours or high for 3 hours.

3. Add pasta and spinach.

4. Cover and cook for a further 30 minutes.

5. Remove bay leaves and season to taste with salt and black pepper. Garnish with micro greens, if desired.

SERVES 4 ★ PREP 10min ★ COOK TIME 3hr LOW

CREAMY CHEESY PASTA

INGREDIENTS

2½ cups (625ml, 20fl oz) whole milk

1½ cups (375ml, 13fl oz) evaporated milk

½ tsp salt

½ tsp pepper

500g (1lb 2oz) spiral pasta

100g (3½ oz) butter

3 cups (375g, 13oz) sharp Cheddar cheese, grated

¼ cup (10g, ¼ oz) fresh parsley, roughly chopped

METHOD

1. In a medium bowl whisk together milk, evaporated milk, salt and pepper.

2. Place the pasta into the slow cooker. Top with butter and cheese. Pour the milk mixture over the top and push pasta down to cover as much as possible. It's okay if it's not completely covered by liquid.

3. Cover and cook on low for 2-3 hours until liquid has absorbed and pasta is cooked. Stir well and serve.

RUSSIAN BORSCHT

INGREDIENTS

Olive oil, for frying

2 onions, finely chopped

4 celery stalks, diced

2 carrots, peeled and diced

4 garlic cloves, minced

1 tsp caraway seeds

½ tsp salt

½ tsp pepper

3 tbsps tomato paste

1 tbsp sugar

3 medium beetroots, peeled and diced

2 small potatoes, peeled and diced

¼ cup (10g, ¼ oz) rosemary leaves (reserve some for garnish)

5 cups (1.25L, 42fl oz) vegetable stock

2 tbsps fresh lemon juice

1 cup (250ml, 8fl oz) sour cream

Rock salt, to garnish

METHOD

1. Heat the oil in a frying pan over medium-high heat. Add onions, celery and carrots, and cook, stirring often, for 5 minutes, until softened.

2. Add the garlic, caraway seeds, salt and pepper and cook for a further 1 minute until aromatic.

3. Transfer the mixture to a medium slow cooker.

4. Add the tomato paste, sugar, beetroot, potato and rosemary. Add the stock and lemon juice. Stir.

5. Cover and cook on low for 8 hours, or on high for 4 hours, or until the vegetables are tender.

6. Ladle soup into bowls and top with the sour cream, rock salt and rosemary leaves, to serve.

MOROCCAN STEW

INGREDIENTS

2 tsps coconut oil

1 large onion, quartered and sliced

2 large potatoes, peeled and cubed

1 tbsp curry powder

½ tsp turmeric

1 tsp ground cumin

1 tbsp light brown sugar

Small piece ginger, peeled and grated

3 garlic cloves, crushed

2 cups (500ml, 1pt) vegetable stock

2 x 400g (14oz) cans chickpeas, drained and rinsed

1 large carrot, halved and sliced

1 small cauliflower, cut into small florets

1 x 400g (14oz) can diced tomatoes

½ tbsp salt

¼ tsp pepper

2 cups (270g, 9oz) kale, roughly chopped

½ cup (125ml, 4fl oz) Greek yoghurt

¼ cup (10g, ¼ oz) fresh parsley, roughly chopped

METHOD

1. Heat the oil in a large frying pan over medium heat. Fry the onion until soft and starting to brown, for about 5 minutes. Add the potatoes and fry for 5 more minutes until just translucent around the edges.

2. Stir in the curry, turmeric, cumin, brown sugar, ginger and garlic, and cook until fragrant, about 30 seconds. Pour in ¼ cup of stock and scrape the bottom of the pan to break up any bits sticking to the bottom. Pour the whole mixture into your slow cooker.

3. Add the rest of the stock, chickpeas, carrot, cauliflower, diced tomatoes with their juices, salt and pepper. Stir to combine. The liquid should come halfway up the sides of the cooker; add more stock if needed. Cover and cook for 3 hours on high.

4. Stir in the kale, cover and cook for a further 1 hour.

5. Season to taste and serve with dollops of yoghurt and garnished with parsley

STUFFED CAPSICUM

INGREDIENTS

6 mixed red, green and yellow capsicums

500g (1lb 2oz) minced beef

½ cup (75g, 3oz) onion, chopped

1 x 400g (14oz) can diced tomatoes

1 cup (165g, 6oz) wild rice, cooked

2 tbsps Worcestershire sauce

1 tsp ground oregano

1 tsp sweet paprika

1 tsp salt

1 tsp pepper

½ cup (50g, 2oz) Parmesan cheese, grated

¼ cup (60ml, 2fl oz) chicken stock

2 tbsps olive oil

METHOD

1. Cut off the tops of the capsicums, reserving the tops, and scrape out the seeds and membranes. Set aside.

2. Place the minced beef, onion, diced tomatoes, rice, Worcestershire sauce, oregano, paprika, salt, pepper and cheese in a large mixing bowl and stir to combine thoroughly.

3. Stuff each capsicum with the mixture and arrange them in the cooker. Put the stock in the bottom of slow cooker and drizzle the oil over the capsicums. Sit the tops on each capsicum.

4. Cook on low for 6 hours or high for 4 hours until the capsicums are tender and the beef is cooked throughout.

ROAST GARLIC AND TOMATO SOUP

INGREDIENTS

1 tbsp olive oil

1 head garlic

1kg (2lb) ripe Roma tomatoes

1 onion, diced

1 x 400g (14oz) can diced tomatoes

1 cup (250ml, 8fl oz) chicken stock

1 tsp salt

½ tsp pepper

1 tsp caster sugar

¼ tsp chilli flakes

¼ tsp cayenne pepper

2 tbsps fresh basil, chopped (retain some for garnish)

½ cup (125ml, 4fl oz) thickened cream

½ cup (60g, 2oz) Parmesan cheese, grated, (retain some for garnish)

METHOD

1. Preheat your oven to 200°C (400°F, Gas Mark 6).

2. Rub olive oil over garlic head. Place in an ovenproof dish with a lid or wrap in aluminium foil. Roast in preheated oven for 25 minutes.

3. Meanwhile, bring a large pot of water to a boil. Add the tomatoes. Boil for 3 minutes. Drain and run under cold water. Peel off skins and discard. Place tomatoes in the slow cooker.

4. Add onion, canned tomatoes, stock, salt, pepper, sugar, chilli flakes, cayenne papper and basil to the slow cooker.

5. Squeeze each clove of garlic to extract the pulp. Discard skins and place pulp in the slow cooker.

6. Cook on high for 3 hours or 6 hours on low.

7. Puree vegetables with a stick blender until completely smooth, or puree in batches in a stand blender. Stir in thickened cream and cheese.

8. Spoon into bowls and top with remaining cheese and basil.

LENTIL TAMARIND SOUP

INGREDIENTS

2 tsps ghee

1 large onion, finely chopped

2 garlic cloves, crushed

1½ tbsps ginger, grated

2 tsps ground cumin

1 tsp ground coriander

½ tsp turmeric

1½ tsps salt, or to taste

2 cups (370g, 12oz) yellow lentils, rinsed and drained

6 cups (1.5L, 50fl oz) water

3 tbsps tamarind concentrate

1 cup (200g, 7oz) tomatoes, seeded and finely chopped

1 x 400ml (14fl oz) can coconut milk

3 tbsps lemon juice

METHOD

1. Heat the ghee in a medium frying pan over medium-high heat.

2. Add the onion and fry for 5 minutes until softened and browned. Add the garlic and fry for a further minute. Stir in the ginger, cumin, coriander and turmeric and stir for 1 more minute until fragrant. Pour in ¼ cup water and stir through then pour all the mixture straight into the slow cooker.

3. Add the rest of the ingredients, cover and cook on low for 8 hours.

4. Season to taste and serve hot.

MEXICAN CORN

INGREDIENTS

3 tbsps butter, softened

1 tsp cayenne pepper

1 tsp ground cumin

1 tsp ground oregano

1 tsp salt

4 large ears of corn

1 lime, cut into wedges

2 tbsps fresh coriander, finely chopped.

METHOD

1. Add the butter to a small bowl and mix through the cayenne pepper, cumin, oregano and salt.

2. Cut four squares of aluminium foil, big enough to wrap each ear of corn completely.

3. Place each ear of corn in the centre of each square of foil. Rub an even amount of flavoured butter over and around each piece of corn. Wrap the pieces of corn up tightly in the foil and place in the bowl of your slow cooker. Turn the slow cooker to low, cover and cook for 4-5 hours.

4. Remove the foil and squeeze over some lime juice and fresh chives to serve.

SERVES 4 ★ PREP 20MIN ★ COOK TIME 7HR LOW/4HR HIGH

LOADED POTATO SKINS

INGREDIENTS

4-6 baking potatoes

1 tbsp olive oil

Salt

Topping

1 tbsp olive oil

280g (10oz) button mushrooms, trimmed and quartered

3 garlic cloves, crushed

Salt and pepper, to taste

¼ cup (10g, ¼ oz) fresh parsley, roughly chopped

⅓ cup (80ml, 3fl oz) vegetable or chicken stock, hot

⅔ cup (160ml, 5fl oz) yoghurt, room temperature

¾ cup (75g, 3oz) Parmesan, finely grated

METHOD

1. Scrub baking potatoes clean and place on a piece of aluminum foil. Drizzle with olive oil and sprinkle with salt. Wrap tightly with foil.

2. Place foil-wrapped potatoes into the slow cooker and cook on high for 4 hours or low for 6-8 hours. Leave on warm until ready to serve.

3. Heat the oil in a large frying pan over medium-high heat. Add mushrooms and garlic and season with salt and pepper. Cook, stirring frequently, for 6-8 minutes or until mushrooms are browned and softened. Stir in the chopped parsley. Set aside.

4. Remove potatoes from slow cooker and cut in half. Scoop out the flesh, leaving a thick edge of potato, and transfer the flesh to a medium bowl. Add the stock and yoghurt to the bowl, season with salt and pepper and stir until combined. Divide this mixture among potato skins, spooning on top of each. Spoon over the mushroom mixture and top with grated cheese.

5. Heat a grill to medium-high. Place potatoes under the grill and cook until cheese has melted.

WHITE BEAN SOUP

INGREDIENTS

470g (1lb) dried cannellini beans

1 tsp olive oil

1-2 rashers bacon, roughly chopped

1 medium onion, diced

1 celery stalk, diced

2 garlic cloves, sliced

3 sprigs thyme (plus extra for garnish)

8 cups (2L, 4pt) chicken stock

Salt and pepper, to taste

¼ cup (5g, ¼ oz) fresh coriander leaves

METHOD

1. To soak the beans, place into a large bowl and cover with water. Set aside overnight.

2. Heat the olive oil in a frying pan over medium heat. Add bacon and fry, stirring, for 1 minute. Add the onion, celery, garlic and thyme leaves. Fry, stirring, for 6-7 minutes or until soft and translucent. Set aside to cool slightly.

3. Drain the beans and place in the slow cooker. Add the bacon mixture, stock, salt and pepper. Cook on high for 3 hours or 6 hours on low.

4. Remove the soup and transfer in batches to a blender. Puree in batches.

5. Season with salt and pepper and garnish with thyme and a couple of coriander leaves.

SPICY RATATOUILLE

METHOD

1. Heat a small frying pan over medium-high heat. Dry fry the pepitas for 3 minutes or until they start to brown. Remove immediately from the pan and set aside.

2. Heat the oil in a large saucepan over medium-high heat. Add the onion and fry for 5 minutes until softened and browned. Add the garlic, chilli flakes and paprika and fry for a further minute. Transfer to the slow cooker.

3. Add the eggplant, zucchini, capsicum, tomatoes, wine and oregano. Cook on low for 3½ hours, stirring once during that time.

4. Turn the cooker to high, then stir through the vinegar. Quickly stir the arrowroot together with ¼ cup of water and slowly pour into the cooker, stirring the contents all the while.

5. Cover, and cook for 15-20 minutes on high.

6. Season with salt and pepper to taste and serve on mashed potato or polenta garnished with the pepitas and parsley.

INGREDIENTS

¼ cup (30g, 1oz) pumpkin seeds (pepitas)

¼ cup (60ml, 2fl oz) olive oil

2 medium onions, halved and sliced

3 large garlic cloves, crushed

1 tsp chilli flakes

1 tbsp smoked paprika

1 small eggplant, quartered and sliced

3 small zucchinis, quartered and sliced

2 large red capsicums, chopped

2 large green capsicums, chopped

1 x 400g (14oz) can diced tomatoes

¼ cup (60ml, 2fl oz) white wine

1 tbsp ground oregano

3 tbsps balsamic vinegar, or more to taste

2 tbsps arrowroot flour

Salt and pepper, to taste

½ cup (20g, ¾ oz) fresh parsley, roughly chopped

MOROCCAN HARIRA SOUP

INGREDIENTS

Olive oil, for frying

1 onion, chopped

2 carrots, sliced

1 tsp ground cumin

1 tsp ground ginger

1 tsp turmeric

½ tsp pepper

6 cups (1.5L, 50fl oz) chicken stock

¼ bunch coriander, leaves chopped, reserving 1 tbsp for garnish

¼ bunch flat-leaf parsley, leaves chopped, reserving 1 tbsp for garnish

1 cinnamon stick

1 cup (185g, 6oz) brown lentils, rinsed

1 x 400g (14oz) can chickpeas, drained

2 x 400g (14oz) cans diced tomatoes

¼ cup (60ml, 2fl oz) lemon juice

METHOD

1. Heat the oil in a frying pan over medium-high heat. Add onion and carrot and fry for 5 minutes, until soft. Add the cumin, ginger, turmeric and pepper and cook for a further 1 minute, stirring, until fragrant. Transfer mixture into a large slow cooker.

2. Add stock, coriander, parsley, cinnamon stick, lentils, chickpeas and tomatoes to the slow cooker and stir to combine.

3. Cover and cook on low for 6 hours, until the vegetables and lentils are tender. Discard the cinammon stick.

4. Stir the lemon juice and reserved chopped herbs into the soup before serving.

COCONUT SOUP WITH QUINOA AND VEGETABLES

INGREDIENTS

1 x 400ml (14fl oz) can coconut cream

4 cups (1L, 2pt) chicken (or vegetable) stock

1 tbsp fresh ginger, minced

2 tbsps green curry paste

1 tbsp fish sauce

1 tbsp palm sugar, grated

1 onion, thinly sliced

1 large sweet potato, peeled and cubed

1 red capsicum, seeded and cut into long strips

1 eggplant, cubed

1 bunch Chinese broccoli, stems and leaves separated and roughly chopped

1 cup (180g, 6oz) fresh edamame soy beans, rinsed and drained (optional)

½ cup (80g, 3oz) quinoa, rinsed and drained

Salt and pepper, to taste

1 tbsp fresh lime juice

2 tbsps chives, chopped, to garnish

2 tbsps coriander, to garnish

4 lime wedges, to serve

METHOD

1. Place all ingredients except lime juice and garnishes in a medium slow cooker.

2. Cover and cook on low for 4 hours, or until the sweet potato is tender.

3. Stir through the lime juice and season to taste.

4. Ladle into bowls and garnish with chives and coriander and place a lime wedge on the side.

VEGETABLE STEW

INGREDIENTS

2 tbsps olive oil

1 large onion, chopped

Salt and pepper, to taste

2 garlic cloves, crushed

1 tbsp ground oregano

2 large Desiree potatoes, peeled and cut into 1cm (½ in) cubes

2 large carrots, cut into 1cm (½ in) cubes

2 small parsnips, peeled and cut into 1cm (½ in) cubes

2 celery stalks, chopped

4 cups (1L, 2pt) vegetable stock

1 cinnamon stick

1 green capsicum, chopped

1 punnet cherry tomatoes, chopped (reserve 6)

200g (7oz) butternut pumpkin, peeled and cubed

1 tbsp apple cider vinegar

2 spring onions, sliced

METHOD

1. Heat the oil in a large frying pan over medium heat. Add the onion and a pinch of salt and cook over medium heat for 5 minutes or until translucent. Add the garlic and oregano and cook for a further minute, until fragrant.

2. Transfer the mixture to a slow cooker. Add the potatoes, carrots, parsnips, celery, stock and cinnamon stick and stir to combine. Cover and cook on high for 1½ hours.

3. Add the capsicum, tomatoes and pumpkin to the slow cooker.

4. Cover and continue to cook on high until the vegetables are tender for 2 hours more, stirring after 1 hour.

5. Just before serving remove the cinnamon stick, stir through the vinegar and season to taste.

6. Cut the reserved cherry tomatoes in half and serve them on the side and garnish the stew with spring onion.

HOMESTYLE BEANS

INGREDIENTS

2 x 400g (14oz) cans cannellini beans, rinsed and drained

Olive oil, for frying

1 large onion, diced

1 medium red capsicum, chopped

4 rashers bacon, chopped

3 cups (750ml, 24fl oz) chicken stock

½ cup (115g, 4oz) passata

1 tbsp apple cider vinegar

½ cup (20g, ¾ oz) fresh basil, finely chopped

¼ cup (40g, 1½ oz) light brown sugar

2 tbsps maple syrup

1 tsp dry mustard

1 tsp Worcestershire sauce

¼ tsp chilli powder

Basil leave, to garnish

METHOD

1. Place beans in a large saucepan and cover with cold water. Bring to a boil and allow to boil, uncovered, for 3 minutes. Remove from the heat, cover and set aside for 1 hour.

2. Heat oil in a large frying pan over a medium-high heat. Add onion, capsicum and bacon and cook, stirring, for 5 minutes until the onion is starting to brown. Reduce heat to medium-low and cook for a further 5 minutes until onion is very soft.

3. Place the beans in the slow cooker.

4. Add stock, passata, vinegar, basil, brown sugar, maple syrup, dry mustard, Worcestershire sauce and chilli powder. Spoon the onion-bacon mixture on top of the bean mixture.

5. Cover and cook on high for 6 hours or low for 8 hours.

6. Season to taste and serve garnished with extra basil leaves.

SPICED PUMPKIN AND CHICKPEA STEW

INGREDIENTS

1kg (2lbs) butternut pumpkin, cut into bite-sized pieces

1 x 400g (14oz) can chickpeas, rinsed and drained

1 large onion, finely chopped

2 garlic cloves, crushed

4 cups (1L, 2pt) vegetable stock

Juice of 1 lime

1 tbsp cumin

1 tbsp ground ginger

1 tsp turmeric

1 tsp nutmeg

1 tsp salt (or more to taste)

½ tsp pepper

¼ cup (10g, ¼ oz) fresh mint, chopped, to garnish

Lime wedges, to serve

METHOD

1. In a large slow cooker, combine all ingredients except the mint and lime wedges. Cover and cook on low for 6-8 hours.

2. Serve each portion with a wedge of lime on the side and garnished with mint.

WILD RICE AND MUSHROOMS

INGREDIENTS

1 tbsp olive oil

2 cups (310g, 8oz) wild rice blend

4 cups (1L, 2pt) vegetable stock

1 cup (150g, 5oz) shallots, finely chopped

450g (1lb) sliced button mushrooms

3 garlic cloves, minced

1 tsp cayenne pepper

2 tsps ground cumin

2 tsps ground oregano

½ cup (20g, ¾ oz) fresh coriander, roughly chopped

2 tbsps lime juice

Salt and pepper, to taste

METHOD

1. Begin by stirring the olive oil with the rice blend until well coated.

2. Add the vegetable stock, shallots, mushrooms, garlic, cayenne, cumin, oregano and half the fresh coriander. Stir until well combined.

3. Cook on low for 5 hours until the rice is tender.

4. Stir through the lime juice and season to taste.

SOFT POLENTA

INGREDIENTS

2 cups (380g, 14oz) polenta

8 cups (2L, 4pt) vegetable or chicken stock

2 tsps salt

1 cup (100g, 3½ oz) Parmesan cheese, grated

2 tbsps butter

400g (14oz) button mushrooms, sliced

1 tbsp mixed dried herbs

Salt and pepper, to taste

4 eggs

¼ cup (60g, 2oz) Greek feta, crumbled

¼ cup (10g, ¼ oz) parsley, roughly chopped.

METHOD

1. Place polenta in a medium slow cooker.

2. Bring water to the boil and pour over the polenta.

3. Add salt and stir well to combine.

4. Cover and cook on low for 6-8 hours or high for 3-4 hours.

5. Stir in cheese 5 minutes before serving.

6. Heat half the butter in a medium frying pan over medium-high heat. Add the mushrooms and herbs and cook for 8 minutes, until browned. Season to taste, remove from the pan and set aside.

7. Add the rest of the butter and fry the eggs to your liking.

8. Serve the polenta topped with mushrooms, feta cheese, parsley and a fried egg.

SEAFOOD AND FISH

Sweet and sour prawns   158
Stuffed squid   159
Prawn, corn and bacon chowder   160
Coconut fish curry   162
Creamy fish soup   163
Prawn and chorizo gumbo   164
Prawn cashew curry   166
Prawn marinara   167
Bouillabaisse   168
Dill baked fish   170
Lemon herb salmon   171
Lobster bisque   172
Tuna casserole   174
Fish pie   175
Prawn risotto   176
Fish stew   178
Mussels in white wine   179
Seafood soup   180
Kedgeree   182
Honey soy salmon   183

SWEET AND SOUR PRAWNS

INGREDIENTS

2 tbsps cornflour

2 tbsps sugar

1 cup (250ml, 8fl oz) chicken stock

1 x 400g (14oz) can pineapple pieces in juice, juice reserved

1 tbsp soy sauce

Small piece ginger, finely minced

2 carrots, peeled and quartered

½ head broccoli, cut into florets

2 spring onions, thinly sliced

1-2 jalapeno peppers (optional)

600g (1lb 5oz) prawns, deveined and peeled

2 tbsps apple cider vinegar

METHOD

1. Combine cornflour and sugar in a small saucepan over medium-high heat. Add chicken stock, ½ cup juice from the canned pineapple, soy sauce and ginger. Bring mixture to a boil, stirring, and cook for 1 minute. Add pineapple pieces and stir to combine. Transfer mixture to a medium slow cooker.

2. Cover and cook on low for 3 hours.

3. Add the carrots, broccoli, spring onions, jalapeno peppers, if using, and prawns and cook for a further 30 minutes, until prawns are pink and cooked through.

4. Add vinegar and stir through before serving.

SERVES 2 ★ PREP 20MIN ★ COOK TIME 2HR 30MIN LOW

STUFFED SQUID

INGREDIENTS

Olive oil, for frying

1 onion, finely diced

2 garlic cloves, minced

¼ tsp paprika

1 tbsp oregano, chopped

1 chorizo sausage, finely diced

½ cup (80g, 3oz) Arborio rice

1 cup (250ml, 8fl oz) fish (or chicken) stock

¼ tsp salt

¼ tsp pepper

4 squid tubes

1 capsicum, seeded and diced

6 tomatoes, roughly chopped

METHOD

1. Heat the oil in a large frying pan over medium-high heat. Add the onion, garlic, paprika and oregano and cook, stirring, for 3-4 minutes until soft. Add the sausage and fry, stirring, for 3-4 minutes until browned. Add the rice and stir to coat. Add the stock, salt and pepper and bring to a gentle simmer for 5 minutes until liquid has evaporated. Set aside to cool slightly.

2. Stuff squid tubes with the mixture, pushing all the way to the end. Secure open end with a toothpick

3. Place capsicum and tomatoes in the bottom of a medium slow cooker. Place the stuffed squid on top.

4. Cover and cook on low for 2½ hours.

5. Check after 2 hours and if necessary to thicken sauce, leave the lid propped open for the final 30 minutes of cooking.

6. Roughly puree the tomato and capsicum sauce with a blender and serve over the squid.

PRAWN, CORN AND BACON CHOWDER

INGREDIENTS

6 rashers bacon, sliced

4 cups (1L, 2pt) chicken stock

1 tbsp butter

5 spring onions, finely chopped

2 cups (350g, 12oz) fresh corn kernels

1 x 400g (14oz) can creamed corn

2 garlic cloves, chopped

½ tsp cayenne pepper

1 tsp salt

400g (14oz) prawns, thawed if frozen

1 cup (250ml, 8fl oz) thickened cream

Spring onion, finely chopped, to garnish

METHOD

1. Fry the bacon in a large frying saucepan over a medium-high heat for 3-4 minutes until cooked.

2. Add the stock, then add butter and spring onions. Stir in corn, creamed corn, garlic, cayenne and salt.

3. Pulse for 30 seconds using a stick blender or pulse in batches using a stand blender.

3. Transfer to the slow cooker.

4. Cover and cook on low for 7 hours on low or 3 hours on high.

5. Add prawns and bacon and cook for a further 1 hour.

6. Stir in cream and then serve, garnished with spring onion.

COCONUT FISH CURRY

INGREDIENTS

2 tbsps coconut oil

2 onions, roughly chopped

3 garlic cloves, chopped

Medium piece ginger, roughly chopped

2 lemongrass stalks, white parts chopped

1 large green chilli, deseeded and chopped

2 tsps curry powder

1 tsp ground turmeric

1 cup (45g, 1½ oz) fresh coriander, chopped (reserve some leaves for garnish)

12 curry leaves

1 x 400ml (14fl oz) can coconut milk

3 cups (750ml, 24fl oz) fish stock

400g (14oz) green beans, trimmed and cut into 3cm (1in) lengths

700g (1½ lb) firm white fish (such as snapper) cut into 3cm (1in) chunks

½ tsp salt

½ lime, juiced

METHOD

1. Place 1 tablespoon coconut oil, half the onion, garlic, ginger, lemongrass, half the green chilli, curry powder, turmeric and half the coriander into a high speed blender and pulse until a coarse paste forms.

2. Melt the rest of the coconut oil in a medium frying pan over medium heat.

3. Fry the remaining onion for about 4 minutes, then pour in the curry paste and cook, stirring, for a further 2 minutes.

4. Add the mixture to the slow cooker with the curry leaves, remaining green chilli, coconut milk, stock and beans.

5. Cover and cook on low for 4 hours.

6. Add the fish and the salt to the sauce, and cook for another ½ hour. Season to taste, gently stir in the lime juice and serve garnished with coriander.

CREAMY FISH SOUP

INGREDIENTS

1 tbsp olive oil

1 small onion, finely chopped

1 small carrot, grated

1 cup (155g, 4oz) short-grain rice

3 garlic cloves, crushed

300g (10oz) potatoes, peeled and cut into 1½ cm (¾ in) cubes

2 cups (500ml, 1pt) vegetable stock

1 tsp celery salt

2 tbsps plain flour

2½ cups (625ml, 20fl oz) full cream milk

600g (1lb 5oz) salmon, skin on, cut into 2cm (1in) pieces

Salt and pepper, to taste

¼ cup (10g, ¼ oz) dill, chopped

METHOD

1. Heat the olive oil in a medium frying pan over medium heat. Add the onion, fry for 5 minutes, until it begins to soften. Then add the carrot, rice and garlic and stir for another minute.

2. Remove the mixture to the slow cooker and add the potatoes, stock and celery salt.

3. Cook on low for 6 hours.

4. Turn the heat to medium, place the flour in a medium bowl and slowly whisk in the milk until the mixture is smooth.

5. Slowly stir the milk mixture into the soup and mix through thoroughly.

6. Add the salmon and cook for 45 minutes or until the salmon is cooked through. Stir after 15 minutes.

7. Season to taste and serve garnished with dill.

PRAWN AND CHORIZO GUMBO

INGREDIENTS

Olive oil, for frying

350g (12oz) chorizo, sliced

2 celery stalks, sliced

1 onion, diced

1 red capsicum, seeded and diced

1 garlic clove, minced

1 tbsp cornflour

1 cup (250ml, 8fl oz) water

1¼ cups (310ml, 10fl oz) chicken stock

1 x 400g (14oz) can diced tomatoes

1 tbsp thyme leaves

2 tsps smoked paprika

455g (1lb) prawns, deveined and peeled, tails intact

1 tbsp parsley, chopped, to garnish

METHOD

1. Heat oil in large frying pan over a medium-high heat. Add chorizo and cook, stirring, for 3-4 minutes untl browned. Drain and set aside. Wipe pan clean with paper towel and heat a little more oil.

2. Add celery, onion and capsicum and cook for 4-5 minutes until almost soft. Add garlic and cook for a further 1 minute until aromatic.

3. Combine cornflour and water in a small mixing bowl to create a slurry, stirring to combine well.

4. Place chorizo and celery-onion mixture in the slow cooker. Pour over the stock and tomatoes. Add thyme and smoked paprika and stir in the cornflour slurry.

5. Cover and cook on low for 3½ hours.

6. Add prawns and cook for a further 1 hour.

7. Serve gumbo over rice, garnished with parsley.

PRAWN CASHEW CURRY

INGREDIENTS

1 tbsp vegetable oil

Small piece ginger, peeled and chopped

6 garlic cloves, chopped

3 tbsps red curry paste

6 ripe tomatoes, roughly chopped

½ cup (60g, 2oz) cashews

2 cups (500ml, 1pt) chicken (or vegetable) stock

4 Asian shallots, quartered

16 green king prawns, peeled and deveined

1 small red chilli, sliced, to garnish

1 spring onion, sliced, to garnish

METHOD

1. Place the oil, ginger, garlic, curry paste, tomatoes and half of the cashews in a blender and pulse until a rough paste forms.

2. Transfer the paste to the slow cooker. Add stock and Asian shallots.

3. Cover and cook on high for 3 hours.

4. Add the prawns and remaining cashews.

5. Cover and cook for 45 minutes, until the prawns are pink and cooked through.

6. Serve in bowls garnished with sliced chilli and spring onion.

PRAWN MARINARA

INGREDIENTS

450g (1lb) fresh or frozen prawns, peeled and deveined

450g (1lb) spaghetti

Parmesan cheese, to garnish

Marinara sauce

1 x 400g (14oz) can diced tomatoes

1 cup (225g, 8oz) tomato passata

¾ cup (185ml, 6fl oz) water

2 garlic cloves, minced

2 tbsps fresh parsley, minced

1 tsp salt

½ cup (20g, ¾oz) basil leaves, chopped

¼ tsp pepper

METHOD

1. In the slow cooker, combine all ingredients for the sauce.

2. Cover and cook on low for 3 hours.

3. Add the prawns. Cover and cook for a further 30 minutes until prawns are pink and cooked through.

4. Cook spaghetti according to the directions on the packet. Drain.

5. Toss marinara sauce through the spaghetti and serve garnished with Parmesan cheese.

BOUILLABAISSE

INGREDIENTS

½ tsp saffron strands

1 cup (250ml, 8fl oz) white wine

1 orange, juiced and zested

Olive oil, for frying

1 onion, diced

1 fennel bulb, trimmed, cored and thinly sliced

2 garlic cloves, minced

1 tsp dried mixed herbs

½ tsp salt

¼ tsp pepper

4 cups (1L, 2pt) fish stock

1 medium tomato, diced

1 bay leaf

500g (1lb 2oz) snapper fillets, cut into bite-sized pieces

350g (12oz) mussels, cleaned and scrubbed

350g (12oz) large king prawns

¼ bunch parsley, chopped

METHOD

1. Soak the saffron strands in a small bowl with the wine and orange juice. Set aside.

2. Heat the oil in a large saucepan over a medium-high heat. Add the onion and fennel and fry, stirring, for 5 minutes until soft. Add the garlic, mixed herbs, salt and pepper and fry for 30 seconds until aromatic.

3. Add the saffron-wine mixture and bring to a gentle boil. Add the fish stock, orange zest, tomatoes and bay leaf and stir to combine. Transfer the mixture to a medium slow cooker.

4. Cover and cook on low for 4 hours.

5. Turn the cooker to high. After 15 minutes, add the fish, mussels and prawns and cook for a further 15 minutes.

6. Discard the bay leaf.

7. Stir in the parsley and serve with crusty bread.

SERVES 6 ★ PREP 15MIN ★ COOK TIME 2HR HIGH

DILL BAKED FISH

INGREDIENTS

6 white fish fillets

¼ cup (60ml, 2fl oz) dry white wine

2 tbsps butter, melted, plus 25g (1oz) butter, room temperature

1 tbsp olive oil

½ lemon, juiced

2 garlic cloves, minced

¼ cup (10g, ¼oz) dill, finely chopped

¼ tsp salt

¼ tsp pepper

METHOD

1. Line the base and sides of the slow cooker inset with aluminum foil, allowing it to cover about halfway up the sides. Place fish on the aluminum foil in one layer and drizzle with white wine, butter, olive oil and lemon juice.

2. Sprinkle garlic, dill and salt and pepper over the fish. Finish with a knob of butter on each fillet. Cover with another piece of foil, tucking in on all sides.

3. Cook on high for 2 hours. Use a fish slice to remove fillets from slow cooker and a spoon to scoop out the juices. Spoon juices over the fish and serve with boiled potaotes and green beans.

SERVES 4 ★ PREP 10MIN ★ COOK TIME 2HR LOW

LEMON HERB SALMON

INGREDIENTS

4 x 200g (7oz) salmon fillets

1 lemon, ½ juiced and ½ sliced

2 tsps cracked pepper

2 tsps dried thyme

2 tsps dried parsley

2 sprigs fresh dill, to garnish

METHOD

1. Lay out a piece of foil twice as big as one salmon fillet. Place a single fillet of salmon on the foil. Repeat with the other 3 salmon fillets. Top the fillets with a lemon juice, pepper, herbs and a couple of lemon slices each. Fold the foil over and crimp edges together, creating an airtight parcel for the fish.

2. Place the foil parcels in the slow cooker, stacked on top of one another if space requires.

3. Cover and cook on low for 2 hours.

4. Remove foil parcels from the slow cooker and carefully open over a plate to catch the juices. Serve garnished with fresh dill.

LOBSTER BISQUE

INGREDIENTS

Olive oil, for frying

½ onion, finely chopped

1 garlic clove, minced

2 x 400g (14oz) cans diced tomatoes

6 cups (1.5L, 50fl oz) chicken stock

1 tbsp celery salt

1 tbsp ground bay leaves

2 tsp pepper

1 tsp paprika

½ tsp dry mustard

¼ tsp ground nutmeg

¼ tsp ground cinnamon

¼ tsp ground cloves

¼ cup (10g, ¼oz) parsley, chopped

4 whole lobster tails

2 cups (475ml, 1pt) thickened cream

Parsley sprigs, to garnish

METHOD

1. Heat oil in a frying pan over medium-high heat. Add onion and fry, stirring, for 5 minutes until soft. Add garlic and cook for a further 1 minute, until aromatic. Transfer to a large slow cooker.

2. Add tomatoes, stock, celery salt, ground bay peaves, pepper, paprika, mustard, nutmeg, cinammon, cloves and parsley to the slow cooker. Stir to combine.

3. With a sharp knife, remove the fan parts at the end of the lobsters and add them to the slow cooker.

4. Cover and cook on low for 6 hours or 3 hours on high.

5. Remove the lobster tail ends from the cooker and discard.

6. Using a stick blender in the slow cooker (or in batches with a stand blender) puree until smooth.

7. Add the rest of the lobster tails to the soup.

8. Cover and cook for 45 minutes on low or until the shells turn bright red.

9. Remove lobster tails from the soup and set aside to cool slightly.

10. Add most of the cream to the soup, retaining a little to finish, and stir.

11. Cut each lobster tail in half lengthways and remove the flesh from the shells. Discard shells, roughly chop lobster meat and return to the soup.

12. Ladle soup into bowls and serve with a dollop of the retained cream and parsley.

TUNA CASSEROLE

INGREDIENTS

1 tbsp butter

4 tbsps flour

2 cups (500ml, 1pt) milk

2½ cups (625ml, 20fl oz) chicken (or vegetable) stock

3 x 185g (6oz) cans tuna in spring water, drained

455g (1lb) penne pasta

1 cup (170g, 6oz) frozen peas

1 cup (175g, 6oz) corn kernels

1 cup (125g, 4oz) mozzarella cheese, grated

1 tbsp oregano, chopped

2 tsps salt

1 cup (100g, 3½ oz) Parmesan cheese, grated

METHOD

1. Melt the butter in a small saucepan over medium heat. Add the flour and stir for 1 minute, until a thick paste forms. Gradually add the milk, stirring constantly. Bring sauce to a gentle boil, stirring, until thickened. Remove the pan from heat and stir in the stock. Set aside.

2. Empty the tuna into a large bowl and break up with a fork. Pour the sauce over top, then add the dry pasta, peas, corn, mozzarella cheese, oregano and salt. Stir to combine. Transfer mixture to a large slow cooker.

3. Cover and cook on low for 2 hours.

4. Sprinkle the Parmesan cheese over the top of the casserole and cook for a further 30 minutes until cheese has melted. If the mixture needs thickening, prop the lid open for the final 30 minutes of cooking.

FISH PIE

INGREDIENTS

3 potatoes, peeled and cubed

2 tbsps butter

4 tbsps flour

2 cups (500ml, 1pt) milk

1 cup (125g, 4oz) Cheddar cheese

3 white fish fillets, cut into small pieces

1 lemon, juiced

1 carrot, grated

2 celery stalks, diced

METHOD

1. Place the potatoes in a large saucepan and cover with salted water. Bring to the boil and cook for 15 minutes until tender. Drain. Return to the pan, add 1 tablespoon butter and mash. Set aside.

2. Melt 1 tablespoon butter in a small saucepan over medium heat. Add the flour and stir for 1 minute, until a thick paste forms. Gradually add the milk, stirring constantly. Bring sauce to a gentle boil, stirring, until thickened. Add cheese and stir until melted. Set aside.

3. Place fish in a large bowl. Pour over the lemon juice and toss. Add carrot and celery, then pour over the sauce. Stir well to combine. Spoon the mixture into a medium slow cooker.

4. Spoon the mashed potato over the top.

5. Cover and cook on low for 3 hours.

PRAWN RISOTTO

INGREDIENTS

90g (3oz) butter

2 tbsps olive oil

1 onion, chopped

2 garlic cloves, minced

2¼ cups (350g, 12oz) Arborio rice

1 cup (250ml, 8fl oz) white wine

2½ cups (625ml, 20fl oz) vegetable stock

Salt and pepper, to taste

455g (1lb) large prawns, deveined and peeled

1 tsp lemon zest

1 tbsp parsley, chopped

1 cup (125g, 4oz) Parmesan cheese, finely grated

⅔ cup (160ml, 5fl oz) thickened cream

¼ tsp cayenne pepper

METHOD

1. Melt the butter and oil in a large frying pan over medium-high heat. Add the onion and garlic and cook, stirring, for 3-4 minutes until soft. Add the rice and stir to coat. Add the wine and bring to a gentle simmer for 3-4 minutes until liquid has almost evaporated. Transfer to the slow cooker.

2. Add the vegetable stock and stir to combine.

3. Cover and cook on low for 1½ hours, stirring regularly. Season to taste with salt and pepper.

4. Add the prawns, lemon zest and parsley and cook for a further 30 minutes until the prawns are pink.

5. To serve, stir in the Parmesan cheese and cream and sprinkle with cayenne pepper.

FISH STEW

INGREDIENTS

2 x 400g (14oz) cans diced tomatoes, undrained

2 onions, chopped

3 celery stalks, chopped

1 red capsicum, seeded and diced

1-2 zucchinis, diced

16 black olives

2 cups (500ml, 1pt) fish (or vegetable) stock

3 tbsps tomato puree

½ cup (125ml, 4fl oz) white wine

4 garlic cloves, minced

1 tbsp red wine vinegar

1 tbsp olive oil

1 bay leaf

½ tsp sugar

½ tsp paprika

450g (1lb) firm white fish, cut into pieces

2 tbsps parsley, chopped

METHOD

1. Place everything apart from fish and parsley into a medium slow cooker.

2. Cover and cook on low for 5 hours.

3. Add fish and cook, covered, for 30 minutes until fish flakes easily with a fork.

4. Remove bay leaf and stir in parsley, then serve.

MUSSELS IN WHITE WINE

INGREDIENTS

450g (1lb) mussels

1 bulb fennel, trimmed, cored and thinly sliced

1 cup (250 mL) dry white wine

2 cups (500ml, 1pt) fish (or chicken) stock

4 garlic cloves, minced

½ tsp salt

¼ tsp pepper

1 tbsp parsley, chopped

¼ cup (60ml, 2fl oz) pouring cream

METHOD

1. Scrub mussels and remove any beards. Set aside.

2. Place fennel, wine, stock, garlic, salt and pepper in a medium slow cooker.

3. Cover and cook on low for 7 hours until fennel is tender.

4. Add mussels and parsley.

5. Cover and cook on high for 15 minutes, until mussels open. Discard any mussels that remain closed.

6. Stir in cream and serve.

SEAFOOD SOUP

INGREDIENTS

2 x 400g (14oz) cans crushed tomatoes

4 cups (1L, 2pt) vegetable stock

½ cup (125ml, 4fl oz) white wine

2 garlic cloves, minced

2-3 new potatoes, cut into bite-sized pieces

3 medium tomatoes, chopped

1 onion, finely diced

1 tbsp fresh thyme

1 handful parsley leaves, roughly chopped (retain a few for garnish)

½ tsp salt

½ tsp pepper

¼ tsp chilli flakes

¼ tsp cayenne pepper

1kg (2lb) mixed seafood (mussels, baby squid, prawns)

METHOD

1. Place all the ingredients except seafood into a large slow cooker.

2. Cover and cook on high for 2 hours or low for 5 hours until potatoes are tender.

3. Add seafood to slow cooker and cook for a further 30 minutes on a high setting.

4. Serve garnished with parsley.

KEDGEREE

INGREDIENTS

550g (1¼ lb) smoked fish

Butter, for frying

1 onion, finely sliced

2 tsps curry powder

2 cups (310g, 8oz) long-grain rice

2 medium tomatoes, chopped

1 tbsp wholegrain mustard

2 tbsps dill, chopped

2 cups (500ml, 1pt) boiling water

2 hard boiled eggs, cut into wedges

2 tbsps sour cream (optional)

Basil leaves, to garnish

METHOD

1. Remove the skin from fish, flake into chunks and set aside.

2. Heat butter in a frying pan over a medium-high heat. Add onion and fry, stirring, for 5 minutes until soft. Add the curry powder and stir for 1 minute or until fragrant. Add rice and fry, stirring, for 2-3 minutes until grains are lightly toasted. Add chopped tomato, mustard and dill and stir to combine.

3. Place the rice mixture into the slow cooker, add boiling water and fish. Stir.

4. Cover and cook on high for 1½ hours.

5. To serve, gently fold through the cream, if using, and place eggs and fish on top of each serving. Garnish with basil.

HONEY SOY SALMON

INGREDIENTS

4 salmon fillets

2 tbsps soy sauce

2 tbsps honey

2 tbsps lemon juice

2 tsps sesame seeds

2 tsps ginger, grated

METHOD

1. Line the base and sides of the slow cooker inset with aluminum foil, allowing it to cover about halfway up the sides.

2. Place fish on the aluminum foil in one layer and drizzle with soy sauce, honey and lemon juice.

3. Cover with another piece of foil, tucking in on all sides.

4. Cook on low for 2 hours.

5. Use a fish slice to remove fillets from slow cooker and a spoon to scoop out the juices.

6. To serve, spoon juices over the fish, sprinkle with sesame seeds and top with a little fresh ginger.

BREAD, CAKES AND DESSERTS

Rosemary loaf   186
Potato buttermilk bread   188
Cornbread   189
Cinnamon rolls   190
Almond banana loaf   192
Rosemary foccacia bread   193
Lemon poppyseed cake   194
Chocolate slice   196
Berry crumble   197
Carrot pineapple cake   198
Candied pecans   200
Chocolate mint fudge   201
Chocolate fudge cake   202
Apple cake   204
Pumpkin cake   205
Creme brulee   206
Bread and butter pudding with brandy sauce   208
Peach cobbler   209
Orange cake   210
Rice pudding   212
Red velvet cake   213
Baked cheesecake   214
Chocolate pudding   216
Gooey brownie cake   217
Sticky date pudding   218
Poached pears   220
Baked apples   221

ROSEMARY LOAF

INGREDIENTS

2 tsps fine polenta

4 tsps active dry yeast

1 tbsp sugar

2 cups (500ml, 1pt) tepid water

4½ cups (560g, 1lb, 2oz) plain flour

1 tbsp fresh rosemary leaves, finely chopped, plus extra rosemary leaves, to garnish

½ tsp salt

2 tbsps olive oil

1 tbsp milk

METHOD

1. Preheat slow cooker on high heat. Remove the inset and grease and dust with the polenta.

2. Place the yeast and sugar into ½ cup of the water and set aside.

3. Place flour in a large mixing bowl and stir through the rosemary and salt.

4. Make a well in the centre and stir in the yeast mixture, the rest of the water and the oil.

5. Mix until it starts to come together to form a dough.

6. Turn the dough out onto a well-floured surface and knead for 10 minutes until it's smooth.

7. Place the dough in the inset and sit it in a warm spot for 5 minutes, covered with a tea towel.

8. Put the inset back in the slow cooker and brush the milk over the top.

9. Bake the bread on high heat for 2 hours 45 minutes or until the sides of the loaf have come away from the sides of the sleeve and the top is browned.

10. Remove the inset and place on a heatproof surface. Let the loaf cool in the inset for 10 minutes, then remove and cool on a wire rack to room temperature.

POTATO BUTTERMILK BREAD

INGREDIENTS

2 potatoes, peeled and quartered

115g (4oz) butter, room temperature

4 tsps active dry yeast

2 cups (500ml, 1pt) buttermilk, room temperature

2 eggs, beaten

2 tbsps sugar

1½ tsps salt

1 tsp fennel seeds

6½ cups (800g, 1¾ lb) strong flour, sifted

METHOD

1. Place potatoes in a saucepan and cover with water. Bring to the boil and cook for 10-12 minutes until fork tender. Drain and roughly mash with a fork.

2. Place potatoes and butter in the bowl of an electric mixer. Add yeast, buttermilk, eggs, sugar, salt and fennel seeds and beat slowly to combine.

3. Gradually add flour and stir until the dough is moist but not sticky.

4. Knead on low to medium speed using the dough attachment, or by hand, until the dough is smooth and elastic.

5. Grease a loaf tin with butter. Gently press the dough into the loaf tin and transfer tin to the slow cooker. (Place a rack or scrunched-up foil on base of slow cooker before putting the tin into the cooker.)

6. Turn the cooker onto high and cook for 1-3 hours. Check with an instant read thermometer after 1 hour, and keep checking every 30 minutes until cooked. When the thermometer reads 90°C (190°F), the bread is ready.

CORNBREAD

INGREDIENTS

2 tbsps butter

1 cup (125g, 4oz) plain flour

1 cup (190g, 7oz) polenta

1½ tbsps sugar

3 tsps baking powder

1 tsp salt

1 cup (250ml, 8fl oz) buttermilk (or milk)

2 eggs

METHOD

1. Place butter in the inset of a large slow cooker. Turn onto high and allow butter to melt.

2. Meanwhile, sift flour over a medium mixing bowl. Add polenta, sugar, baking powder and salt. Then add buttermilk and eggs and stir to combine.

3. Pour the cornbread batter into the slow cooker and smooth the surface evenly with a spatula or knife.

4. Cover and cook on high for 2 hours.

CINNAMON ROLLS

INGREDIENTS

¾ cup (185ml, 6fl oz) milk

2¼ tsps instant yeast

¼ cup (55g, 2oz) plus 1 tsp caster sugar, divided

1 tsp salt

3 tbsps butter, melted

1 egg

2½ cups (310g, 10oz) plain flour

Vegetable oil, for brushing

Flling

70g (2½ oz) butter, room temperature

1 tbsp ground cinnamon

⅓ cup (70g, 2½ oz) caster sugar

Icing

1¼ cup (195g, 6½ oz) icing sugar

1 tsp vanilla extract

2 tbsps milk

METHOD

1. In a small saucepan, warm the milk over low heat. Pour the warm milk into the bowl of a stand mixer fitted with the dough hook attachment (or use a handheld mixer).

2. Stir in the yeast and 1 teaspoon sugar. Cover with a towel and allow to sit for 5-10 minutes until foamy. (If not foamy, try again with fresh yeast).

3. On low speed, beat in the remaining sugar, salt, butter, egg and flour until a soft dough forms.

4. Turn the dough out onto a lightly floured surface. Knead for 2 minutes. Cover and set aside to rest for 10 minutes.

5. Line a medium slow cooker with baking paper. Brush a little oil on the baking paper.

6. Roll out the dough to a rectangle about 18 x 10cm (7 x 4in). Spread the softened butter on top, and sprinkle the cinnamon and sugar over the surface of the dough. Roll up tightly, then cut into 10 even pieces.

7. Place rolls inside the lined slow cooker. Stretch a clean, dry tea towel over the slow cooker and then put the lid on. This will absorb the excess moisture.

8. Cook on low for 2 hours. Remove from slow cooker by lifting out the baking paper.

9. Whisk the icing sugar, vanilla and milk together until smooth. Dilute with more milk if required. Drizzle over the warm rolls.

ALMOND BANANA LOAF

INGREDIENTS

1 cup (125g, 4oz) plain flour

1 tsp bicarbonate of soda

1 tsp salt

1 cup (120g, 4oz) almond meal

½ cup (60g, 2oz) almonds, roughly chopped (retain 1 tbsp to decorate)

125g (4oz) butter, room temperature

1 cup (155g, 5oz) brown sugar

2 eggs

1 tsp vanilla extract

3 large ripe bananas, mashed

METHOD

1. Lightly grease the inset of a large slow cooker or grease a loaf tin.

2. Sift flour, bicarb and salt over a bowl. Add almond meal and almonds and stir to combine. Set aside.

3. Using a hand mixer or in the bowl of an electric mixer, beat butter and sugar until fluffy. Add eggs, one at a time, beating well after each addition. Stir in vanilla and the mashed bananas. Gradually add dry ingredients, stirring until the mixture is moist.

4. Pour batter into the slow cooker or the prepared tin. Smooth surface using a spatula and push retained almonds into the top. (If using a loaf tin, place a rack or scrunched-up foil on base of slow cooker before putting the tin into the cooker.)

5. Cover and cook on high for 2½ hours (if cooking in the inset itself) or 3½ hours if cooking in the loaf tin, until a skewer inserted in the centre comes out clean.

SERVES 6 ★ PREP 10MIN ★ COOK TIME 1HR HIGH

ROSEMARY FOCCACIA BREAD

INGREDIENTS

3 cups (375g, 12oz) self-raising flour

2 cups (500ml, 1pt) warm water (or less)

1 tsp of salt

2 sprigs rosemary, leaves picked and finely chopped (retain 1 tsp for garnish)

½ tsp rock salt, to serve

METHOD

1. Line the slow cooker with baking paper, so that the paper extends slightly above the top of the bowl.

2. Sift the flour over a large mixing bowl. Add water, salt and rosemary and stir well until a thick dough forms. Add more flour if needed to achieve this.

3. Place the dough in the slow cooker.

4. Stretch a clean, dry tea towel over the slow cooker and then put the lid on. The tea towel will absorb the excess moisture.

5. Cook on high for 1 hour.

6. Remove from the slow cooker and brown the top under the grill for 5 minutes.

7. Sprinkle with rock salt and retained rosemary to serve.

LEMON POPPYSEED CAKE

INGREDIENTS

210g (8oz) butter, room temperature

1¼ cups (275g, 10oz) caster sugar

2 eggs

2 cups (500ml, 1pt) sour cream

1 tsp vanilla extract

1 lemon, zested and juiced

1½ tbsps poppy seeds

1¾ cups (215g, 7oz) plain flour

½ cup (100g, 3oz) polenta

1 tsp baking powder

1 tsp bicarbonate of soda

¼ tsp salt

Glaze

1½ cups (235g, 8oz) icing sugar

4 tbsps lemon juice

METHOD

1. In the bowl of an electric mixer, beat the butter and sugar together until pale and creamy. Beat in the eggs, one at a time, beating for 1 minute after each addition. Add the sour cream, vanilla, lemon zest and poppy seeds and beat for a further 1 minute.

2. In a separate medium bowl, combine the flour, polenta, baking powder, bicarb and salt.

3. Slowly add dry ingredients to the wet ingredients and mix on low until just combined.

4. Grease and line the base and sides of a medium, round slow cooker with baking paper, leaving an overhang at the top. (You can also use a greased cake tin and place into the inset of the slow cooker.) Pour the batter into the lined slow cooker inset or cake tin. Stretch a clean, dry tea towel over the slow cooker and then put the lid on. This will absorb the excess moisture.

5. Cook on high for 2½ hours, or until a skewer inserted into the centre comes out clean.

6. To make the glaze, whisk icing sugar and lemon juice together.

7. Remove the cake using the baking paper and transfer to a wire rack to cool for 20 minutes before serving.

8. Drizzle with glaze to serve.

SERVES 8 ★ PREP 15MIN ★ COOK TIME 3HR LOW (PLUS COOLING)

CHOCOLATE SLICE

INGREDIENTS

1½ cups (185g, 6oz) flour

¼ cup (30g, 1oz) cacao powder

¾ tsp baking powder

1 cup (220g, 8oz) caster sugar

½ tsp salt

125g (4oz) butter

1½ cups (235g, 8oz) dark chocolate chips

3 eggs, room temperature, lightly beaten

1 tsp vanilla extract

METHOD

1. Take 2-3 sheets of heavy-duty aluminium foil, folded several times, and line the inside of a large slow cooker. Place a piece of baking paper inside the foil base.

2. Sift the flour, cacao and baking powder over a large mixing bowl. Add sugar and salt and stir to combine.

3. Place butter and chocolate chips in a small heatproof bowl over a pan of simmering water and cook, stirring, until chocolate is smooth and melted.

4. Pour chocolate into the dry ingredients and gently fold to combine. Add eggs and vanilla and stir until smooth.

5. Transfer batter to slow cooker. Cover and cook on low for 3 hours. Uncover and allow to cool in the slow cooker for 1 hour.

6. Remove by pulling baking paper out of the slow cooker.

BERRY CRUMBLE

INGREDIENTS

150g (5oz) fresh or frozen blueberries

100g (3½ oz) fresh or frozen cranberries

200g (7oz) fresh or frozen boysenberries

¼ cup (40g, 1½ oz) brown sugar

1 tsp lemon juice

1¼ cups (110g, 3¾ oz) steel cut rolled oats

½ cup (60g, 2oz) macadamias, finely chopped

½ cup (60g, 2oz) plain flour

1 tsp cinnamon

1 tsp allspice

¼ tsp ground cloves

Pinch of salt

¼ cup (80g, 3oz) pure maple syrup

4 tbsps unsalted butter, room temperature, cubed

METHOD

1. Grease the inside of the slow cooker.

2. Toss the berries together with the brown sugar and lemon juice then place them in an even layer in the bottom of the slow cooker.

3. In a separate mixing bowl, stir together the rolled oats, macadamias, flour, cinnamon, allspice, cloves and salt.

4. Drizzle over the maple syrup and scatter over the pieces of butter.

5. Use a large knife or spatula and use chopping motions to combine the mixture until it becomes crumbly with larger clumps throughout.

6. Layer the crumble over the berries in the slow cooker.

7. Cover and cook on low heat for 4 hours.

8. Serve warm.

CARROT PINEAPPLE CAKE

INGREDIENTS

1 x 225g (8oz) can crushed pineapple

1½ cups (235g, 8oz) packed brown sugar

2 eggs

½ cup (125ml, 4fl oz) vegetable oil

1 tsp vanilla extract

¼ cup (60ml, 2fl oz)

2 cups (250g, 8oz) plain flour

2 tsps baking powder

2 tsps cinnamon

1 tsp bicarbonate of soda

½ tsp salt

½ tsp nutmeg

2 medium carrots, grated

Cream cheese icing

250g (9oz) cream cheese, softened

65g (2oz) butter, softened

½ tsp vanilla

1 cup (155g, 5oz) icing sugar

6 walnuts, halved, to decorate

¼ cup (40g, 1½oz) candied pineapple, to decorate

METHOD

1. Grease and line the base and sides of a large slow cooker with baking paper, leaving an overhang at the top.

2. Drain the pineapple with a fine-mesh sieve. Set aside.

3. In a large mixing bowl, beat together sugar, eggs, oil, vanilla and water until smooth.

4. Sift flour, baking powder, cinnamon, bicarb, salt and nutmeg over a medium bowl.

5. Add wet ingredients to dry ingredients, then add carrot and pineapple and stir until mixture is all wet.

6. Scrape into the slow cooker, smoothing the surface with a spatula. Cover and cook on high for 2 hours, or until a skewer inserted in the centre comes out clean.

7. Turn off slow cooker. Uncover and allow to cool in the slow cooker for 30 minutes.

8. Lift the cake out using the baking paper and set aside on a wire rack to cool completely.

9. Meanwhile, in the bowl of an electric mixer, beat cream cheese, butter and vanilla until smooth. Gradually add icing sugar, and beat until smooth.

10. Spread icing over the top of the cooled cake and decorate with walnuts and candied pineapple.

CANDIED PECANS

INGREDIENTS

¾ cup (165g, 6oz) caster sugar

½ cup (80g, 3oz) light brown sugar

1½ tbsps cinnamon

1 egg white

2 tsps vanilla

5 cups (625g, 1lb 6oz) pecans

¼ cup (60ml, 2fl oz) water

METHOD

1. Combine the sugar, brown sugar and cinnamon in a large mixing bowl. Set aside. In a separate bowl whisk together egg white and vanilla until frothy.

2. Lightly grease the inset of the slow cooker. Place pecans inside and pour over the egg white mixture. Stir until nuts are evenly coated. Sprinkle the cinnamon-sugar mix over the top and stir again to coat the nuts well.

3. Cover and cook on low for 3 hours. Stir every 20 minutes or so. Twenty minutes before cooking time is finished, add the water into the slow cooker and stir. Remove from cooker and spread nuts out onto a baking tray to cool for 15 minutes before serving.

SERVES 8 ★ PREP 15MIN ★ COOK TIME 1HR 10MIN HIGH

CHOCOLATE MINT FUDGE

INGREDIENTS

2 cups (310g, 10oz) milk chocolate chips

¼ cup (60ml, 2fl oz) whipping cream

⅓ cup (105g, 4oz) maple syrup

½ cup (80g, 3oz) white chocolate chips

1 tsp peppermint essence

Sea salt, to serve

METHOD

1. Place the milk chocolate chips, whipping cream and maple syrup into the slow cooker. Cover and cook on high for 1 hour. Leave on the lid and don't peak!

2. After an hour, place the white chocolate chips into the slow cooker and stir until melted. If necessary, cover for ten minutes and then stir again. Add the peppermint essence and stir. When all ingredients are combined and melted, pour the mixture into a baking dish lined with greaseproof paper. Set aside for 2-3 hours or until completely cooled. Cut into squares and sprinkle with sea salt.

   Note: Store in airtight container at room temperature.

CHOCOLATE FUDGE CAKE

INGREDIENTS

1½ cups (170g, 6oz) unsweetened cocoa powder

1 cup (125g, 4oz) plain flour

2 tsps baking powder

¼ tsp salt

2 tbsps butter, melted

2 eggs, room temperature

½ tbsp vanilla extract

1 cup (155g, 5oz) sugar

½ cup (115g, 4oz) plain Greek yogurt

¾ cup (185ml, 6fl oz) milk

Frosting

500g (1lb 2oz) dark chocolate, finely chopped

1 cup (250ml, 8fl oz) thickened cream

2 tbsps sugar

5 tbsps unsalted butter

METHOD

1. Lightly grease a round cake tin that fits inside your slow cooker with butter.

2. Sieve the cocoa powder, flour, baking powder and salt over a medium bowl.

3. In a separate bowl, whisk together the butter, eggs and vanilla. Add the sugar, yogurt and half of the milk and mix well to eliminate any lumps. Add half of the flour mixture and stir until just incorporated. Add the remainder of the milk and stir to combine. Add the remainder of the flour and stir until just incorporated. Don't over mix.

4. Scrape the batter into the prepared tin. Place in the slow cooker and cook on low for 2½ hours, or until the centre is just firm to the touch.

5. Remove the lid, turn off the slow cooker, and cool the cake in cooker for 10 minutes, then remove and transfer to a wire rack to cool completely.

6. Meanwhile, place the chocolate in a large bowl. In a small saucepan, bring cream and sugar to a boil. Pour over the top of the chocolate and leave to stand for 5 minutes. Gently whisk until smooth. Add the butter and whisk until incorporated. Refrigerate for 30 minutes or until thick enough to spread.

7. Slice cake in half crossways and fill and top with the frosting.

APPLE CAKE

INGREDIENTS

1 cup (220g, 8oz) caster sugar

¹/₃ cup (40g, 1½ oz) plain flour

¹/₃ cup (40g, 1½ oz) self-raising flour

¹/₃ cup (50g, 2oz) cornflour

Pinch salt

2 apples, cored, peeled and grated

1 tbsp lemon zest

4 eggs, room temperature, separated

1 tbsp unsalted butter, melted

¼ cup (60ml, 2fl oz) milk

2 tbsps icing sugar

METHOD

1. In a large mixing bowl, mix together sugar, flours and salt and make a well in the centre.

2. Drain and squeeze the grated apples to remove excess liquid.

3. Add the zest, apple, egg yolks, butter and milk and stir to combine thoroughly.

4. Beat the egg whites until stiff peaks form. Gently fold them into the apple mixture, using a slotted spoon. Try to keep the batter as light as you can.

5. Pour into the cooker and cook on high for 2 hours or until a skewer inserted into the middle comes out clean. It should be light and fluffy and golden.

6. Turn out onto a wire rack to cool and sift the icing sugar over the top.

PUMPKIN CAKE

METHOD

1. Take 2-3 sheets of heavy-duty aluminium foil, folded several times, and line the inside of a large slow cooker. Place a piece of baking paper inside the foil base.

2. Using an electric mixer, beat together butter and sugar until creamy. Beat in eggs one at a time until thoroughly combined. Add vanilla extract. Beat in pumpkin.

3. Fold in the flour, baking powder, bicarb, spices, and salt until a smooth batter forms.

4. Pour into prepared slow cooker.

5. Cover and cook on high for 3 hours (check at 2 hours) or until a skewer inserted in the centre comes out clean.

6. Use the baking paper to lift cake from the slow cooker and allow to cool for 20 minutes before serving.

INGREDIENTS

125g (4oz) butter, softened

2 cups (310g, 10oz) brown sugar, packed

3 eggs

2 tsps vanilla extract

2 cups (450g, 1lb) pumpkin, cooked

1½ cups (185g, 6oz) plain flour

1½ tsps baking powder

1½ tsps bicarbonate of soda

1 tsp cinnamon

¼ tsp nutmeg

¼ tsp ground ginger

Pinch of ground cloves

½ tsp salt

CREME BRULEE

INGREDIENTS

1½ cups (375ml, 13fl oz) thickened cream

½ cup (125ml, 4fl oz) full cream milk

1 tsp vanilla extract

6 small egg yolks, room temperature

⅓ cup (70g, 2½ oz) caster sugar

1½ tbsps caster sugar, for torching

Pinch of salt

METHOD

1. Lightly oil four ramekins with a light oil such as vegetable or canola.

2. Place the cream, milk and vanilla into a medium saucepan over medium-high heat and bring to a boil. Remove from the heat, cover with a tight-fitting lid and sit for 15 minutes.

3. Whisk together the egg yolks and half the sugar in a large mixing bowl until smooth and light in colour. Gradually add the cream until completely mixed through.

4. Divide the mixture between the four ramekins, then gently place them in the bottom of the slow cooker. Fill the cooker with enough hot water to come almost up to the tops of the ramekins.

5. Bake for 2½ hours on low heat or until the creme brulees are set.

6. Remove them from the cooker and let them sit for 1 hour, then cover them with plastic wrap and place in the refrigerator to chill for at least 2 hours.

7. Just before serving, sprinkle the rest of the sugar over the top of each creme brulee. Use a kitchen torch to melt the sugar until it forms a slightly browned crispy top.

BREAD AND BUTTER PUDDING WITH BRANDY SAUCE

INGREDIENTS

Pudding

8 large thick slices of day-old white sourdough bread

60g (2oz) butter, room temperature

1 cup (160g, 6oz) sultanas

2 cups (500ml, 1pt) full cream milk

4 medium eggs, room temperature

60g (2oz) butter, melted

½ tsp cinnamon

¼ cup (55g, 2oz) caster sugar

½ tsp vanilla extract

¼ tsp ground nutmeg

Brandy sauce

60g (2oz) butter

3 tbsps plain flour

⅔ cup (100g, 3oz) light brown sugar

1 cup (250ml, 8fl oz) milk

¼ cup (60ml, 2fl oz) brandy

¼ tsp vanilla extract

METHOD

1. Butter the sourdough with butter and break the bread up into rough chunks. Layer the bread and sultanas in the bottom of the cooker.

2. Whisk the rest of the pudding ingredients together in a mixing bowl, then pour the mixture over the bread.

3. Stretch a tea towel over the top of the slow cooker and then put the lid on. Cook on low for 4 hours until cooked through and a skewer inserted in the middle comes out clean.

4. To make the sauce, first melt the butter in a small saucepan over medium heat. Mix the flour and sugar together then stir into the butter. Slowly pour in the milk, whisking continously. When smooth and almost boiling, stir in the brandy and vanilla.

5. Remove from heat and serve with the pudding.

PEACH COBBLER

INGREDIENTS

8 fresh clingstone peaches, peeled and sliced, or 4 cups (600g, 1lb 5oz) tinned peaches, drained

115g (4oz) butter, room temperature

1 cup (220g, 8oz) caster sugar

1 large egg, beaten

½ tsp vanilla extract

1 cup (125g, 4oz) plain flour

½ tsp baking powder

1 tsp cinnamon

¼ tsp allspice

METHOD

1. Lightly grease the slow cooker.

2. Arrange the peaches in the bottom.

3. In a medium mixing bowl, beat together butter and sugar until they resemble whipped cream.

4. Add egg and vanilla and mix through until thoroughly combined.

5. Add the flour, baking powder, cinnamon and allspice to the mixture in thirds, mixing well after each addition.

6. Spread the batter over the peaches.

7. Stretch a tea towel over the top of the slow cooker and then put the lid on. This will absorb the excess moisture.

8. Cover and cook on high for 2½ hours.

9. Serve hot with cream or ice cream.

ORANGE CAKE

INGREDIENTS

Cake

2 tbsps light brown sugar

2 small oranges, cut into 3mm (⅛ in) thick slices and pips removed

115g (4oz) butter, room temperature

1¼ cups (275g, 10oz) caster sugar

3 large eggs, room temperature

3 tbps orange zest

2 tsps orange juice

1 tbsp Cointreau

1 cup (125g, 4oz) plain flour

½ tsp baking powder

½ tsp bicarbonate of soda

1 cup (120g, 4oz) almond meal

½ tsp salt

1 cup (250ml, 8fl oz) full cream milk

Syrup

1 cup (250ml, 8fl oz) fresh orange juice, strained

1 cup (220g, 8oz) caster sugar

METHOD

1. Grease the inset of the slow cooker, then line with greased baking paper. Sprinkle the brown sugar over the base and arrange the orange slices over the base in overlapping concentric rings.

2. Beat the butter together with the caster sugar until it looks like whipped cream. Beat in the eggs one at a time, making sure each one is completely mixed through before adding the next. Then mix through the the orange zest, juice and Cointreau.

3. In a separate bowl, sift the flour together with the baking powder and bicarb. Stir through the almond meal and salt.

4. Add the flour and the milk in thirds to the egg mix, combining both in well after each addition until you have a smooth batter.

5. Pour the batter into the lined slow cooker inset. Stretch a tea towel over the top of the slow cooker and then put the lid on. This will absorb the excess moisture.

6. Cook on high for 2½ hours, or until a skewer inserted into the centre comes out clean.

7. To make the syrup, heat the orange juice and sugar in a small saucepan over medium-high heat until simmering. Reduce the heat to low and simmer for 15 minutes, stirring to dissolve any sugar.

8. Once the cake is cooked, poke holes in it with a skewer or toothpick and pour the syrup over the top. Let it soak into the cake for 20 minutes before carefully lifting the cake in the baking paper out of the inset and then inverting onto a serving plate.

RICE PUDDING

INGREDIENTS

¾ cup (120g, 4oz) short-grain white rice

3 cups (750ml, 24fl oz) full cream milk

1 cup (250ml, 8fl oz) coconut milk

½ cup (110g, 4oz) caster sugar

½ tsp vanilla paste

Pinch of salt

2 tbsps unsalted butter

1 small egg, room temperature, lightly beaten

6 cinnamon sticks (optional)

1 tsp cinnamon

METHOD

1. Rinse the rice 3 times in cold water or until the water from the rice runs clear.

2. Lightly grease the slow cooker sleeve.

3. Place the rice, milk, coconut milk, sugar, vanilla and salt into the cooker and gently stir to combine.

4. Cook on high for 2½ hours.

5. Remove ¼ cup of the mixture from the pudding and mix the butter through it. Then add it to the egg and quickly whisk it through.

6. Whisk the egg mixture back through the rest of the rice.

7. Cover and cook for ½ hour more.

8. To serve, divide the pudding between six serving bowls, place a cinnamon stick in each bowl and dust with cinnamon.

RED VELVET CAKE

INGREDIENTS

2¼ cups (280g, 10oz) plain flour

1 tsp bicarbonate of soda

1 tsp baking powder

1 tsp salt

2 tbsps cacao powder

200g (7oz) butter

1¾ cups (385g, 14oz) caster sugar

2 tsps vanilla extract

2 large eggs, room temperature

1 cup (250ml, 8fl oz) buttermilk

1 tsp apple cider vinegar

½ cup (125ml, 4fl oz) hot coffee

¼ cup (50ml, 2fl oz) red food colouring

Icing

500g (1lb 2oz) cream cheese

175g (6oz) butter, room temperature

¼ tsp vanilla extract

4 cups (620g, 1lb, 4 oz) icing sugar, sifted

METHOD

1. In a large bowl sift together the flour, bicarb, baking powder, salt and cacao powder.

2. In a separate mixing bowl cream together the butter and sugar until it resembles whipped cream. Add the vanilla and eggs and beat in gradually, one egg at a time.

3. Stir in the flour mix and when combined stir through the buttermilk and vinegar. Lastly stir in the coffee and add small amounts of red food colouring until you get a shade of red that you like.

4. Line the slow cooker with greased baking paper. Pour the cake mix into the cooker. Place a clean tea towel over the top of the cooker to absorb moisture and place the lid on top.

5. Cook on high for 3 hours. Uncover and let cool in the cooker for 1 hour and then lift out onto a wire rack.

6. Whisk together the icing ingredients until light and fluffy and use to ice the cake once cool.

BAKED CHEESECAKE

INGREDIENTS

¾ cup (75g, 3oz) Granita biscuits, crushed

2½ tbsps unsalted butter, melted

¼ tsp mixed spice

⅔ cup (140g, 5oz) caster sugar

Salt

350g (12oz) cream cheese, room temperature, cubed

1 cup (250ml, 8fl oz) creme fraiche

1 tbsp plain flour

2 large eggs, room temperature

1 tsp vanilla paste

1 tsp finely grated lime zest

METHOD

1. In a medium bowl, mix the Granita biscuit crumbs with the butter, mixed spice, 1 tablespoon of the sugar and a pinch of salt. Press the mixture into the bottom of a deep and round 15cm (6in) springform cake tin (or whichever size tin will fit into your slow cooker.)

2. Place the cream cheese, creme fraiche and flour into the bowl of a stand mixer and beat for 1 minute. Pour in the rest of the sugar and a pinch of salt and beat for 2 more minutes until smooth.

3. Add the eggs one at a time as well as the vanilla and lime zest. Once the eggs are thoroughly incorporated, beat for another 30 seconds.

4. Pour the mixture into the cake tin and smooth over the top.

5. Place a tea towel in the bottom of the cooker and place the cake tin on top. Pour enough water into the cooker to come 2cm (1in) up the sides of the tin.

6. Stretch another tea towel over the top of the cooker, cover and cook the cheesecake for 2 hours on high. Turn off the slow cooker and let the cake cool inside the cooker for another 1 hour. Don't remove the lid during the cooking or cooling time.

7. Remove the tin from the cooker, transfer the tin to a wire rack to cool to room temperature.

8. Refrigerate the cake for at least 3 hours before removing from the tin and serving.

CHOCOLATE PUDDING

INGREDIENTS

1 tbps unsalted butter, for greasing ramekins

1½ cups (185g, 6oz) self-raising flour

1 cup (220g, 8oz) caster sugar

90g (3oz) unsalted butter, softened

½ tsp vanilla paste

4 tbsps cacao powder, divided

1 large egg, room temperature, lightly beaten

¾ cup (185ml, 6fl oz) full cream milk

1 cup (155g, 5oz) brown sugar

2½ cups (625ml, 20fl oz) boiling water

1½ tbsps icing sugar, for dusting

METHOD

1. Preheat the slow cooker for 20 minutes on high.

2. Grease 6 small ramekins with butter, or 4 large ramekins, depending on what your slow cooker can hold.

3. Sift the flour into a large mixing bowl, then whisk in caster sugar, butter, vanilla paste, 2 tablespoons cacao powder, egg and milk. Mix everything well then divide the batter between the ramekins.

4. Sprinkle the brown sugar and remaining 2 tablespoons cacao powder over the top of the puddings.

5. Place the ramekins in the bottom of the slow cooker. Then gently pour the boiling water over the top of each. Pour extra water into the bottom of the slow cooker to come halfway up the sides of the ramekins.

6. Cook on high for 3 hours.

7. Remove the ramekins and dust the tops with icing sugar.

8. Serve warm.

GOOEY BROWNIE CAKE

INGREDIENTS

180g (6oz) unsalted butter, room temperature

1 cup (220g, 8oz) caster sugar

½ cup (80g, 3oz) light brown sugar

⅔ cup (70g, 2½ oz) cacao powder

⅓ cup (40g, 1½ oz) plain flour

½ cup (60g, 2oz) slivered almonds, roughly chopped

3 large eggs, room temperature, lightly beaten

¼ tsp ground cardamom

½ tsp vanilla paste

Pinch of salt

¾ cup (120g, 4oz) milk chocolate, roughly chopped

METHOD

1. Grease the sleeve of a slow cooker and line with greased baking paper.

2. Melt the butter, then place in a large mixing bowl with the sugars, cacao, flour, almonds, eggs, cardamom, vanilla paste and salt.

3. Mix everything together until just mixed through then gently fold in the chocolate pieces.

4. Pour the brownie batter into the prepared pan and smooth the top over.

5. Cover and cook on low heat for 3 hours until the brownie is cooked, but still just a bit gooey in the middle.

6. Serve warm with ice cream on the side.

STICKY DATE PUDDING

INGREDIENTS

Pudding

1½ cups (260g, 9oz) Medjool dates, pitted and chopped

2 tsps bicarbonate of soda

¼ cup (60ml, 2fl oz) boiling water

2½ cups (310g, 10oz) plain flour

2 tsps baking powder

1 tsp allspice

½ tsp cinnamon

Pinch of nutmeg

1 cup (155g, 5oz) light brown sugar

1¼ cups (310ml, 10fl oz) full cream milk

50g (2oz) unsalted butter, melted

Sauce

4 cups (1L, 2pt) boiling water

¾ cup (120g, 4oz) light brown sugar

75g (3oz) unsalted butter, chilled and cubed

METHOD

1. Preheat the slow cooker to low heat.

2. Mix the dates with the bicarb and water in a small bowl. Stir to dissolve the bicarb and set aside.

3. Sift the flour, baking powder and spices into a large mixing bowl. Add the sugar and stir to mix everything through then make a well in the centre.

4. Mix together the milk and melted butter. Stir the milk into the flour mixture in thirds, stirring well before making the next addition.

5. Once combined, stir through the dates and their liquid until well combined. Set aside.

6. In a medium saucepan, whisk together the water, sugar and butter until the sugar is dissolved and the butter has melted. Pour into the slow cooker.

7. Drizzle the cake batter over the sauce in an even layer.

8. Cover and bake for 3 hours or until a skewer inserted into the centre of the pudding comes out clean.

9. The sauce will be thick and in the bottom of the slow cooker.

10. Serve hot with sauce and cream or ice cream.

POACHED PEARS

INGREDIENTS

6 firm Buerre Bosc pears

½ cup (80g, 3oz) packed light brown sugar

⅓ cup (115g, 4oz) honey

2 tbsps Cointreau

1 tbsp unsalted butter, melted

2 tsps orange zest, finely grated

¼ tsp ground cardamom

1 tbsp arrowroot flour

3 tbsps orange juice

METHOD

1. Peel the pears and leave stems intact, then sit them upright in the bottom of the cooker.

2. Mix together the rest of the ingredients except the arrowroot and orange juice.

3. Pour the mixture over the pears.

4. Cook, covered, on high heat for 2 hours 45 minutes until the pears are tender. Remove the pears and place in pre-warmed individual dessert bowls.

5. Keep the cooker on high heat. Mix together the arrrowroot and orange juice and pour into the remaining liquid in the cooker. Stir for 15 minutes or until the sauce has thickened to desired consistency.

6. Spoon the sauce over the pears and serve them warm.

BAKED APPLES

INGREDIENTS

½ cup (80g, 3oz) light brown sugar

¼ cup (30g, 1oz) almonds, chopped

2 tbsps sultanas

½ cup (60g, 2oz) fresh or frozen cranberries

2 tsps cinnamon

6 red apples (gala or pink lady), cored

2 tbsps Cointreau (optional)

2 tbsps butter

½ cup (125ml, 4fl oz) apple juice

METHOD

1. In a large bowl, mix together the sugar, almonds, sultanas, cranberries, and cinnamon.

2. Use a sharp paring knife to cut a shallow well about a quarter of the way into the top of the apple. Finely chop the apple that you've removed and add to the fruit mixture.

3. Spoon the filling into the apples and place the apples in the bottom of the slow cooker.

4. Pour the Cointreau over the top of each apple then press a small amount of the butter into the top of each.

5. Pour the apple juice into the bottom of the slow cooker.

6. Cover and cook the apples on high for 3 hours until the apples are cooked through.

7. Serve warm.

INDEX

almonds
almond banana loaf 192
apple
apple cake 204
baked apples 221
pork and apple stew 42
spiced apple butter 64
apricot
apricot chicken 89
banana
almond banana loaf 192
barley
barley risotto with mushroom
and pumpkin 126
vegetable barley nourishing
bowls 117
beans
bean and vegetable enchiladas 122
beef taco soup 10
homestyle beans 150
minestrone soup 132
Tex-Mex chicken soup 78
white bean soup 144
beef
beef bourguignon 24
beef brisket ragu 8
beef goulash 35
beef stroganoff 15
beef taco soup 10
Belgian beef stew 18
cabbage rolls 125
chilli con carne 32
corned beef 26
easy pot roast 34
French veal stew 12
hearty beef stew 20
Irish stew 27
Italian meatballs 14
Korean ribs (galbi jjim) 30
lasagne 11
massaman curry 19
Mongolian beef 31
osso bucco 28
Philadelphia sandwich 23
sausage and tortellini soup 16
sloppy joes 22
stuffed capsicum 137
beetroot
Russian borscht 134
berries
berry crumble 197
brandy
bread and butter pudding with
brandy sauce 208

cabbage
cabbage rolls 125
capsicum
chicken drumsticks with capsicum
99
spicy ratatouille 145
stuffed capsicum 137
sweet and sour chicken 106
carrot
carrot pineapple cake 198
honey glazed carrots 128
vegetable and ham soup 61
vegetable stew 149
cauliflower
Moroccan stew 136
cheese
baked cheesecake 214
creamy cheesy pasta 133
ham, egg and cheese tart 62
chicken
apricot chicken 89
Cajun chicken with rice 85
chicken and mushroom pot pies
90
chicken cacciatore 81
chicken coconut curry 82
chicken drumsticks with capsicum
99
chicken stroganoff 88
chicken taquitos 94
chicken teriyaki 108
chicken tikka masala 102
chicken with rice and sultanas 104
chicken with tomatoes and
herbs 98
coq au vin 84
farmhouse chicken broth with
dumplings 110
glazed duck with figs 100
homemade chicken stock 103
honey BBQ chicken tacos 86
honey rosemary chicken 76
maple dijon chicken 109
Moroccan lemon chicken 92
orange sesame drumsticks 80
paprika chicken 95
red chicken curry 96
sweet and sour chicken 106
Tex-Mex chicken soup 78
Vietnamese chicken pho soup 74
whole roast chicken 77
chickpeas
Moroccan harira soup 146
Moroccan stew 136

spiced lamb and chickpea stew 66
spiced pumpkin and chickpea
stew 152
chilli
beef taco soup 10
chilli con carne 32
Vietnamese chicken pho soup 74
chocolate
chocolate fudge cake 202
chocolate mint fudge 201
chocolate pudding 216
chocolate slice 196
gooey brownie cake 217
red velvet cake 213
cinnamon
cinnamon rolls 190
rice pudding 212
coconut
chicken coconut curry 82
coconut fish curry 162
coconut soup with quinoa and
vegetables 148
corn
bean and vegetable enchiladas 122
Mexican corn 141
prawn, corn and bacon
chowder 160
curry
chicken coconut curry 82
chicken tikka masala 102
coconut fish curry 162
easy lamb madras 54
massaman curry 19
prawn cashew curry 166
red chicken curry 96
dates
sticky date pudding 218
eggplant
spicy ratatouille 145
eggs
ham, egg and cheese tart 62
Spanish tortilla 114
fish
bouillabaisse 168
coconut fish curry 162
creamy fish soup 163
dill baked fish 170
fish pie 175
fish stew 178
honey soy salmon 183
kedgeree 182
tuna casserole 174
garlic
roast garlic and tomato soup 138

roast lamb with garlic and
    rosemary 38

ham
    ham, egg and cheese tart 62
    pea and ham soup 60
    vegetable and ham soup 61

honey
    honey BBQ chicken tacos 86
    honey glazed carrots 128
    honey rosemary chicken 76
    honey soy salmon 183

lamb
    easy lamb madras 54
    lamb rogan josh 51
    lamb shanks in gravy 55
    lamb shanks in red wine sauce 69
    roast lamb with garlic and
        rosemary 38
    spiced lamb and chickpea stew 66

lemon
    lemon herb salmon 171
    lemon poppyseed cake 194
    Moroccan lemon chicken 92

lentils
    healthy lentil casserole 116
    lentil tamarind soup 140
    Moroccan harira soup 146

lobster
    lobster bisque 172

milk
    creme brulee 206
    rice pudding 212

mint
    chocolate mint fudge 201

mushrooms
    barley risotto with mushroom
        and pumpkin 126
    chicken and mushroom pot
        pies 90
    Marsala mushrooms 124
    vegetable barley nourishing
        bowls 117
    wild rice and mushrooms 153

mussels
    bouillabaisse 168
    mussels in white wine 179
    seafood soup 180

orange
    orange cake 210
    orange sesame drumsticks 80

pasta
    creamy cheesy pasta 133
    lasagne 11
    minestrone soup 132

pork ragu 43
prawn marinara 167
sausage and tortellini soup 16
tuna casserole 174

peach
    peach cobbler 209

pear
    poached pears 220

peas
    pea and ham soup 60

pecans
    candied pecans 200

pineapple
    carrot pineapple cake 198
    sweet and sour chicken 106
    sweet and sour prawns 158

plum
    plum jam 65

polenta
    cornbread 189
    soft polenta 154

pork
    banh mi sandwich 58
    Chinese roast pork (char siu) 47
    glazed pork meatballs 44
    meatballs in tomato sauce 68
    pork and apple stew 42
    pork ragu 43
    pork tenderloin with rice pilaf 70
    pulled pork 52
    slow-cooked pork ribs 48
    slow-roast pork shoulder 56
    sweet and spicy pork shoulder 46
    sweet easy pork casserole 40

potato
    loaded potato skins 142
    potato buttermilk bread 188
    slow roast potatoes with dill 120
    spanish tortilla 114
    vegetable and ham soup 61
    vegetable barley nourishing
        bowls 117
    vegetable stew 149

prawns
    bouillabaisse 168
    prawn and chorizo gumbo 164
    prawn cashew curry 166
    prawn, corn and bacon
        chowder 160
    prawn marinara 167
    prawn risotto 176
    seafood soup 180
    sweet and sour prawns 158

pumpkin
    barley risotto with mushroom
        and pumpkin 126
    pumpkin cake 205
    pumpkin risotto 118
    pumpkin soup with roasted
        hazelnuts 130
    spiced pumpkin and chickpea
        stew 152

quinoa
    coconut soup with quinoa and
        vegetables 148
    quinoa with vegetables 121

rice
    Cajun chicken with rice 85
    chicken with rice and sultanas 104
    kedgeree 182
    pork tenderloin with rice pilaf 70
    prawn risotto 176
    pumpkin risotto 118
    rice pudding 212
    stuffed capsicum 137
    wild rice and mushrooms 153

rosemary
    honey rosemary chicken 76
    rosemary foccacia bread 193
    rosemary loaf 186

sausage
    prawn and chorizo gumbo 164
    sausage and tortellini soup 16
    sausage jambalaya 50

squid
    seafood soup 180
    stuffed squid 159

sultanas
    bread and butter pudding with
        brandy sauce 208

tamarind
    lentil tamarind soup 140

tomato
    chicken cacciatore 81
    chicken with tomatoes and
        herbs 98
    homestyle tomato sauce 129
    meatballs in tomato sauce 68
    minestrone soup 132
    roast garlic and tomato soup 138

veal
    French veal stew 12

zucchini
    spicy ratatouille 145
    vegetable barley nourishing
        bowls 117

First Published in 2018 by Herron Book Distributors Pty Ltd
14 Manton St
Morningside
QLD 4170
www.herronbooks.com

Custom book production by Captain Honey Pty Ltd
12 Station St
Bangalow
NSW 2479
www.captainhoney.com.au

Cataloguing-in-Publication. A catalogue record for this book is available from the National Library of Australia

ISBN 978-0-947163-75-4

Printed and bound in China by 1010 Printing International Limited

5 4 3   19 20 21 22

NOTES FOR THE READER

Preparation, cooking times and serving sizes vary according to the skill, agility and appetite of the cook and should be used as a guide only.

All reasonable efforts have been made to ensure the accuracy of the content in this book. Information in this book is not intended as a substitute for medical advice. The author and publisher cannot and do not accept any legal duty of care or responsibility in relation to the content in this book, and disclaim any liabilities relating to its use.

PHOTO CREDITS

Front cover: AS Food studio
Back cover: Kiian Oksana
A. Zhuravleva p207. Africa Studio p123. alisafarov p94, 98, 165. alohadave p217. AnastasiaKopa p163. Anastasia_Panait p33. Aneta_Gu p161. AnikonaAnn p44. Anna Hoychuk p140. Anna Shepulova p121, 211. Arina P Habich p102. AS Food studio p25,56,69,89,110,111. Avdeyukphoto p208. Barbara Dudzinska p15. Bastiaanimage stock p22. Brent Hofacker p27, 28, 37, 38, 49, 63, 141, 185, 189, 216, 222, 234. Dani Vincek p71, 170. Dar1930 p53. Daxiao Productions p246, Digivic p199. Elena Demyanko p233. Elenadesign p88. Elena Mayne p61. Elena Shashkina p179. Family Business p241. Farbled p81. flashgun p249. FOOKPHOTO.COM p251. from my point of view p19,118. getideaka p23. Grezova Olga p230.GuzelKam p183. Heike Rau p213. hlphoto p43, 77, 105, 182, 193, 204. Igor Dutina p39. Irina Rostokina p135, 175. istetiana p229. Joannawnuk p173. Joe Gough p196. Joshua Resnick p93,190. Julia Sudnitskaya p219. Katarzyna Hurova p76. Kate Grigoryeva p70. Kiian Oksana p9, 73, 75. Lara Uster p174. Lesya Dolyuk p225. Let Geo Create p32. Liliya Kandrashevich p11. Lucky_elephant p243. Magdanatka p201 Maggiezhu p59. marco mayer p181. margouillat photo p155. Mariontxa p139. marmo81 p45. Martin Turzak p13, 164. marysckin p31, 65, 117, 129, 159, 169, 187. merc67 p237. minadezhda p231.MShev p119. MSPhotographic p66. naito29 p101. Nataliya Arzamasova p85, 131. Nickichen p223. olepeshkina p215. Olga Nayashkova p137. Olga Miltsova p35. Olha Afanasieva p127. OnlyZoia p138. Pawel Strykowski p205. photosimysia p132. preecha2531 p191. Ramon grosso dolarea p87. Robyn Mackenzie p57,115. Ronald Sumners p29. sarsmis p99, 145, 153. Scruggelgreen p83. SEAGULL_L p50, 55, 147. Sea Wave p1, 2, 6, 40, 78, 124, 176. Seeme p247. SGM p227. Slawomir Fajer p21. Stepanek Photography p91. Stephanie Frey p235. stockcreations p17. stocksolutions p67. Stolyevych Yuliya p151. successo images p97. Tatiana Volgutova p221. Tatiana Vorona p200, 239 teleginatania p149. Teri Virbickis p167. thefoodphotographer p253. travellight p51, 95, 99, 103. Victoria Kondysenko p133. Vladislav Noseek p245. White78 p195. Wiktory p109,197. yingko p107. Yulia Davidovich p203. zi3000 p143. ziashusha p157. zoryanchik p113
Images used under license from Shutterstock.com
p47, © Yvonne lee harijanto Unsplash